teach® yourself

**personal safety
and self defence**

teach®
yourself

personal safety
and self defence
robert g. ross

Launched in 1938, the **teach yourself** series grew rapidly in response to the world's wartime needs. Loved and trusted by over 50 million readers, the series has continued to respond to society's changing interests and passions and now, 70 years on, includes over 500 titles, from Arabic and Beekeeping to Yoga and Zulu. What would you like to learn?

be where you want to be with **teach yourself**

For UK order enquiries: please contact Bookpoint Ltd, 130 Milton Park, Abingdon, Oxon, OX14 4SB. Telephone: +44 (0) 1235 827720. Fax: +44 (0) 1235 400454. Lines are open 09.00–17.00, Monday to Saturday, with a 24-hour message answering service. Details about our titles and how to order are available at www.teachyourself.co.uk

For USA order enquiries: please contact McGraw-Hill Customer Services, PO Box 545, Blacklick, OH 43004-0545, USA. Telephone: 1-800-722-4726. Fax: 1-614-755-5645.

For Canada order enquiries: please contact McGraw-Hill Ryerson Ltd, 300 Water St, Whitby, Ontario, L1N 9B6, Canada. Telephone: 905 430 5000. Fax: 905 430 5020.

Long renowned as the authoritative source for self-guided learning – with more than 50 million copies sold worldwide – the **teach yourself** series includes over 500 titles in the fields of languages, crafts, hobbies, business, computing and education.

British Library Cataloguing in Publication Data: a catalogue record for this title is available from the British Library.

Library of Congress Catalog Card Number: on file.

First published in UK 2007 by Hodder Education, part of Hachette Live UK, 338 Euston Road, London, NW1 3BH.

First published in US 2007 by The McGraw-Hill Companies, Inc.

This edition published 2007.

The **teach yourself** name is a registered trade mark of Hodder Headline.

Typeset by Transet Limited, Coventry, England.
Printed in Great Britain for Hodder Education, an Hachette Livre UK Company, 338 Euston Road, London NW1 3BH, by Cox & Wyman Ltd, Reading, Berkshire.

The publisher has used its best endeavours to ensure that the URLs for external websites referred to in this book are correct and active at the time of going to press. However, the publisher and the author have no responsibility for the websites and can make no guarantee that a site will remain live or that the content will remain relevant, decent or appropriate.

Hachette Livre UK's policy is to use papers that are natural, renewable and recyclable products and made from wood grown in sustainable forests. The logging and manufacturing processes are expected to conform to the environmental regulations of the country of origin.

Impression number   10 9 8 7 6 5 4 3 2
Year   2010 2009 2008

contents

Disclaimer

While this book is designed to provide accurate information with regard to its subject matter, it is not intended as a substitute for qualified legal advice. Due to the author's experience, the law referred to in this book is predominately UK law; however, this does not mean that the advice given herein is not applicable worldwide.

The author and publisher take no responsibility for accident, injury or any other consequence of following the advice and techniques herein. Students practise at their own risk.

acknowledgements

The author would like to acknowledge and thank the following people for their useful contributions, assistance and efforts in bringing this publication together:

Peter Bartlett, Frances Inglis, Euan Ross, Patrick McGovern, Katy Cousins, John Mowat, Ian Storrar, Duncan Roberts and the publishing team at Hodder Education.

Robert Ross was born and educated in Dundee. He is an internationally renowned self defence tutor, having travelled the world teaching and coaching self defence techniques. He has a Masters degree in Ju Jitsu (eighth Dan) and has been inducted into four martial arts halls of fame for Ju Jitsu and sports medicine. He has a degree in sport science and is a sports therapist at the Dundee sports medicine centre, which he established in 1987. Before becoming a director of performance and coaching and a self defence coach and coach tutor at the Scottish Ju Jitsu association, Robert also served as a police officer for over ten years.

introduction

You only have to read the daily newspapers to see that violent crimes occur. We owe it to ourselves and to our loved ones to be able to protect them and ourselves in the instance of a hostile or violent attack. By increasing your awareness you can become more vigilant and prevent incidents occurring. Crimes of violence range from abuse, bullying, assault, rape and murder to smaller, but nevertheless harmful, instances of physical harm. Violent behaviour can occur virtually at any time and at any place without warning, although circumstances usually alert you to its possibility. It can happen from those whom you'd least expect, such as a relative or a friend, and irrespective of whether it's from a spouse, a child, other relative or a friend, there is no justification for violent, aggressive behaviour.

Purpose

The purpose of this book is to raise your awareness so that, first, you are in a better position to predict when a dangerous situation may arise and prevent and manage this situation; and, second, if you are ever put in immediate danger, you can recall the essential self defence techniques and put them into practice. Self defence is not about winning. It's not a competition. It's all about **personal safety**, raising awareness and learning strategies to cope with potentially dangerous situations.

This book is divided essentially into two parts: the first part will improve your self awareness and help you deal with aggression and conflict management. It includes over 100 suggestions for increasing your personal safety and, by including them in your daily life, they will become as automatic as answering the telephone when it rings. These first chapters detail all you'll need to know about becoming assertive or improving your assertiveness and include some useful exercises to help you on your way. Improving your assertiveness is absolutely fundamental to raising your own level of personal safety; and it is a skill that may prevent and certainly manage a very dangerous situation, and one you should keep with you throughout your life. The second part of this book is highly practical and helps you develop physical skills to cope in a variety of situations. It includes technical information to deepen and broaden your understanding.

Programme of physical protocols

Good self defence is about learning how to avoid violence and how to cope with the stress, the fear, the shock and chaos of an attack. I have designed a self defence programme for you containing 20 physical protocols, detailed in Chapter 05, to help you learn how to cope with physical attacks. We will go through it step by step to maximize your success. The most important thing to remember is that you have choices to make. Generally speaking you have four options and you should apply them in this order:

1 avoid violent situations
2 run away
3 talk your way out of the situation
4 use physical violence to escape.

You should note the distinct difference between using physical violence to escape and using physical violence to engage in a brawl.

The self defence techniques in our programme rely on your being attacked first. In this way you act defensively opposed to the aggressors: those who make the attack. There are very few times when it is necessary to make a **pre-emptive attack** as a means of de-escalation, but be alert to this method of dealing with aggressive confrontation – covered in Chapter 06. My approach is to help you tailor the protocols to suit you and build into your programme a number of characteristics that indicate potential success. Our programme shows you how to despatch an aggressor from a variety of common situations and how to escape to safety. The techniques will be small in number, but they will be highly efficient. We will go through your programme using a step by step method, making the techniques easy to learn and, provided you follow and practise them, easy to recall.

These techniques form only a part of your overall approach to self defence and give you ownership of what you do rather than simply responding because someone said do this or do that. This is motivational and serves to raise your confidence and self-esteem. It is important that you feel good about yourself and that your abilities increase as a consequence of these steps. The physical protocols must also be easy to recall during practice or training. I will help you make the correct associative links to ensure success. At the end of each technique there is a summary of the points you'll need to remember and some coaching tips to help you improve. Learning the physical self defence protocols can take some practice but it should be fairly straightforward for everyone. The hallmark of good self defence techniques is ease of recollection and application – they are also designed to build your confidence.

In our programme there are four golden rules to learning self defence, although these are not strictly speaking rules, but rather guidelines based on best practice. These rules are:

1 having the right frame of mind
2 steering away from complications and keeping things simple
3 using only reasonable force if you do have to use your skills
4 realizing that you should only do so when there is no other way out.

The physical protocols chapter applies these four rules in a number of common attack scenarios.

Power of practice

It will be important to practise the techniques in the self defence section (Chapter 05). Select a friend or a relative you can trust, someone who will take the practice seriously. Having a practice partner to share ideas with as well as the ups and downs of learning something new will be an invaluable asset. By practising the techniques, you will develop the co-ordination, accuracy and control needed for real action. Practice also aids your recall and, ultimately, you won't have to rely solely on your memory but more on a sensory feel for all the components. If you ever have to use the techniques you won't have to think about what to do, you'll just react appropriately. Taking the time to practise helps you overcome your initial fears and paves the way to self-confidence.

Self defence is not just about avoiding violence but also involves coping with the stress and shock of an attack. People who learn and practise self defence are not averse to using their skills if and when necessary, but equally they are not 'have a go heroes'. They are decent people who are vigilant and aware of their surroundings and know when to beat a hasty retreat.

There is a big difference between fighting and self defence. Fighting involves two or more consenting individuals engaging in combat with the intention of causing each other physical harm. Loosely speaking, self defence is a legal term set out by Lord Widgery in 1969, which was used as a plea in mitigation. Over the years society has adopted it to describe actions or preparations we can take to defend ourselves and our rights in the event of an attack. In Chapter 06 we examine just what the law's view is on this matter and see just how this relates to our daily lives.

Self defence is not a martial art

Undertaking self defence in a modern world has a great value to anyone provided the physical protocols are relevant to the environment around them. There is little point in learning moves and tricks that will never happen or indeed are so complex that they might require choreography to work. They may look good, even flashy, but they have little value in a real situation. I refer specifically to the martial arts and other combat forms. Many people relate learning self defence to learning highly skilful martial arts such as karate, judo, boxing, etc. and this may be due to the role played by the media in extolling these, but nothing could be further from the truth. These combative forms tend to be complicated and may have a competitive, spiritual or personal development bias to them. While not wishing to knock these forms, they are not strictly **self defence systems**. There is a distinct difference between a system built specifically for the purposes of self defence and a system that has components that can be modified to work in the same or similar circumstances. Many people do not want all the 'frills or trimmings' that martial arts provide and would rather just have what is colloquially known as the 'no nonsense version'.

I repeat, self defence is not about winning. It is not a competition! Remember, self defence is all about personal safety, raising awareness and learning strategies to cope with potentially dangerous situations. Mostly, self defence involves little or no physical skill whatsoever, but it does involve the use of some brainpower.

Dangerous jobs

Some people have jobs that carry inherent dangers, for instance, those who work alone in a shop, social workers, prison officers, traffic wardens, policemen – the list goes on. Some of these occupations are so dangerous that many employers actually train their employees to deal with situations in a particular way, whether that be to minimize liability for the company or to increase the safety of the employee. However, one interesting point is that companies and employers have a responsibility to provide their staff with suitable training should their duties involve putting them at risk of attack, for example, through house calls. If you have a job that fits this description then ask your employer whether self defence training can be provided. You might find your employer sympathetic to your needs. This book will start you off by detailing a basic programme. The 'Taking it further' section at the back of the book may help you find an avenue to further your study or find an accredited self defence coach if you feel you'd like to learn more. Be aware, though, that there are no sure-cure methods of safety to completely eliminate dangerous situations from your life. Our environment is so varied that rules for safety are really only basic guidelines, which need to be shaped according to the lifestyle we choose. Accordingly, you may well have to make a few rules of your own and your ability to maintain a flexible ownership and strong approach to your rules will be the very foundation of your success.

The overall message throughout this book is to be aware of your surroundings, use good common sense and never forget to be a decent human being.

Bob Ross

01

aggression and assertiveness

In this chapter you will learn:
- how to identify aggression
- how to handle a bully and potentially violent face-to-face situations
- how to become assertive by learning assertiveness skills.

When all around you are losing their heads, it is important that you keep yours. If you understand what causes aggression and violence you are halfway to overcoming them. This chapter shines light on aggression and how to become assertive. Becoming assertive is important to your well-being as well as your personal safety. Allowing yourself to be treated like a proverbial doormat causes both your emotional and your mental fitness to deteriorate.

What is aggression?

Human aggression is instinctive; it is part of our makeup. Popularly, it's seen as an externalization or expression of the negative feelings we experience, often at the centre of a conflict. Interpreting aggressive behaviour can be very tricky, because not all aggressive behaviour is deemed to have intent on harming another. Mostly it is an expression of frustration from either irresolvable conflict or as a learned coping mechanism. Aggressive behaviour was thought at the beginning of the twentieth century to be the domain of men, but this is no longer considered the truth. Both sexes can display aggressive behaviour equally. In fact, modern society has in many ways facilitated the expression of aggressive behaviour by promoting ways to vent aggression, for example at sporting events such as football matches or rallies and public protests, etc.

Aggressiveness is, in the context of this book, considered to mean that someone expresses their rights but at the expense, degradation or humiliation of someone else. Aggression can be internalized or externalized. Externalization of aggression would involve physically aggressive behaviour displayed outwardly to others. Internalization of aggression results in a spectrum of feelings from frustration to, ultimately, self-harming. Aggression can be so emotionally or physically forceful that the rights of others are not allowed to surface. It can be true that those who are passionate about a particular thing or subject can express themselves aggressively in this way. However, the physical expression might not have any intent and be nothing more than a wanton act.

One common factor of aggressiveness is that it usually results in others becoming angry or vengeful towards the perpetrator. There are consequences that can work against the perpetrator's best intentions causing others to lose respect for him/her. The perpetrator may well feel self-righteous or superior at that specific moment but on review of the situation might well feel guilty about their actions.

There are also some people who are characteristically 'aggressive' and never see themselves as anything other than right. The major stumbling block here is that displays of aggression are usually twinned with anger. These two components can prevent anyone from acting and thinking reasonably. This can have the effect of decreasing one's ability to use good judgement and therefore impair your overall effectiveness.

It has been well documented that consuming alcohol can reduce your inhibitions and give you the 'Dutch courage' to say and do things you might not normally say or do. Alcohol also clouds and distorts your judgement and perception of reality. Because of these effects, avoiding alcohol is certainly a positive step if you are prone to aggressive behaviour.

Bullying

Bullying is a very hurtful act perpetrated by anyone from childhood through to adulthood and, left unchecked, can cause major problems. It can happen anywhere humans interact and is often described as part of the pecking order within the species. Indeed it can sometimes be difficult to determine what is bullying and what is a justifiable expression of authority. Bullying is endemic in our schools because we are forcibly thrust together during our formative years and during this time of our lives we experimentally learn about social rules and their consequences. During any school term, almost 60 per cent of all school children experience bullying in one form or another. Bullying is not limited to children. It occurs between adults and also between adult and child too.

There are two main types of bully:

- those who act on their own and prey on others
- those who need others to support them.

Both are predatory, but the main difference is that the former is usually bigger in stature and often has a position of authority or assumed authority. This type can be found at work or at school, colleges or other public institutions.

The latter type of bully needs others to support him/her during the execution of bullying activities. This is their crutch, for without the crowd behind them it would be questionable whether they would have the nerve. These individuals are generally smaller than their victims, insecure and can be quite spiteful in their acts. These, too, can be found anywhere, including in the workplace, at home or places of recreation.

Boy bullies may use physical threats such as: *Give me your dinner money or I'll beat you up* whereas girl bullies tend to use psychological or social threats such as: *I won't be your friend if you don't let me have your ...* or *I'm going tell everyone you are a common slut if you...*

It is well known that bullies left to conquer will eventually alienate everyone, except other bullies. Research over the years has revealed it is very likely that if this behaviour is left unchecked the future direction of bullies will be towards anti-social behaviour, abusive behaviour and more serious crimes.

Bullies at work will often force you into doing things you'd rather not do by perhaps telling you that your job is at stake or some such similar ploy. Strangely enough, the bullying displayed in adolescence does not manifest itself that differently in adulthood other than in, perhaps, a slightly more refined way. For example you can still be 'sent to Coventry' (isolated), there may be name calling, rude, brash or offensive behaviour in your presence and much more, all in the workplace.

There are a number of agencies across the length and breadth of the country that work diligently to help those who suffer from bullying. Some of these agencies are listed at the back of this book in 'Taking it Further'.

How to handle a bully

- Avoid them like the plague. Don't be in their company or near them.
- Be assertive: *Leave me alone or I will inform my parents/ teacher/the police/supervisor/HR department.* Don't use empty threats – follow them up.
- Seek people: **safety is in numbers.** Build yourself a small group of friends who will give you support. Bullies normally act when you are at your most vulnerable and when they are least likely to get caught. Be aware that in a group it is very easy to slip into the same behavioural patterns as a bully by seeking revenge or retribution.

- Learn the techniques (physical protocols) contained in Chapter 05.
- Role play to gain and increase confidence.
- Seek advice from your parents, school councillor, etc.

Ethnic and racial slurs

These days most companies have policies that prevent racial abuse at work, particularly if the company has a mixture of races within its workforce. If a company fails to act on a complaint, major action can be taken against the company for allowing it to happen as well as against the perpetrator. Jokes at the expense of others are not jokes at all. Joking about someone's ethnicity or cultural background, religion or personal appearance cannot be considered as acceptable and you should report such matters to the appropriate authorities. These jokes may appear harmless but they are, in fact, harmful. Abuse of anyone is not acceptable and if it is racially motivated this is simply an aggravation of the offence. Do not accept it... report the issue.

How to handle potentially violent face-to-face situations

It is believed that violence and aggression are linked in the brain. Whether we are dealing with children or adults the essence of this is the same. Imagine the brain as having two parts, one part called the **primitive brain** and the other the **rational brain**. The primitive brain is responsible for feeling all emotions such as love, hate, anger, envy, greed, jealousy, etc. The rational brain has the job of working out how to get the primitive brain what it wants. This is normally governed by obeying the rules, customs and rituals of society – but not exclusively so. In a face-to-face situation, confrontation is unavoidable, but it is manageable. Knowing how to make good use of your verbal and nonverbal skills will be the key to success. To do this you communicate with your assailant's primitive brain – play to its basic needs and utilize verbal strategies – say the right things. Every good police negotiator knows these tricks and I am ready to share them with you.

If you start with the correct attitude and posture you'll avoid the traps in body language. The chapter in this book dealing with communication skills (Chapter 03) provides you with the tools you'll need for success. It is just as important to know how and what to say to defuse or talk your way out of a situation. (See the section on telling a lie in Chapter 03.)

Some verbal strategies you might use are: giving reassurance – *I understand how this looks but everything can turn out okay*; making an apology – *I'm sorry, I didn't mean for that to happen*; facing the person down; remaining silent to provoke the other person to make a first response; asking for the required behaviour. Other strategies you might deploy are: playing for time, delaying compliance with a request, causing a conversational diversion or depersonalizing the issue. They can all be tailored to your needs. Role playing with a trusted friend is an excellent way to practise these strategies and hone your skills without anyone actually being in any danger.

When role playing consider how you feel when you carry out your part. Imagine you are taking part in a play where you can stop the action and analyse things before continuing. How would you like it to turn out? What changes can you make to elicit the result you desire? Finally, give yourself some feedback. How did you do? Were you successful in achieving your goal? If not, what adjustments might you make to change the outcome? How did you feel about yourself and about your performance? No matter how bad a situation turns out there are always options. Consider the following:

- How might you make your escape or withdrawal? Would you make an excuse or hit and run?
- How would you call for help? Would you simply shout or use the phone or tap out a message on a pipe?
- What action would you take if attacked? Would you roll over and play possum or are you prepared to stand your ground and fight? Would you run?
- What action would you take if someone else is attacked? Will you shout, will you intervene or call for help?

It is clear that you have choices to make. It may be easy for me to tell you to do this or do that but my approach is about **empowering you** to accept ownership for your decisions. In each of these options you need to focus on and judge what to do and when. If you are attacked you should think about shouting back at your attacker, calling for help, drawing attention to yourself, seeking people or running.

What is assertiveness?

Assertiveness is the ability to express yourself and your rights without violating the rights of others (see Appendix 1 for examples of your rights). Many people have difficulty speaking up or expressing themselves in certain situations. Some feel intimidated by pushy people or have low self-esteem and regularly cast aside their own desires in favour of what others want. A lack of assertiveness can make you feel powerless and can lead you to feel depressed or lower your self-esteem even more.

1 Do you often find that others coerce you into thinking their way?
2 Is it difficult for you to express your positive or negative feelings openly and honestly?
3 Do you sometimes lose control and become angry at others who don't warrant it?

If you answered **yes** to any of these questions it may point to a lack of assertiveness. This is a situation you **can** change. Developing assertiveness skills can help you to manage interpersonal situations more effectively and feel better about yourself in those situations. Part of developing your assertiveness may require you to make certain changes to your attitude or your behaviour. This helps you judge when it is reasonable and appropriate to stand your ground, rather than giving in to others. It is **not** about being aggressive.

One of the first things to do when developing assertiveness skills is to identify why you allow yourself to be treated in a negative way. This involves examining your feelings – how do you feel when you are in an uncomfortable situation? – and, depending on the result, you may need to make some changes to either counter these sensations or understand and accept them.

You are in a bar and a stranger approaches, sits beside you and starts to strike up a conversation. Consider how you feel and do something about it. You can either get up and walk away making your excuses or you can stay and chat. How you feel will determine your action.

You are in the supermarket and in the next aisle are some people you know, but they are unaware of your presence. You happen to be the topic of their very unpleasant diatribe. Do you confront them or do you make yourself scarce? Remember, it's easy to say

Yeah, I would confront them… but think about what you would say,
how you would say it and what body language you would use.

Your employer has called you to the main company office to
accept an award and when you arrive you find yourself in the
centre of television cameras and journalists from the press. They
all want to interview you. This was totally unexpected and you are
not sure how to respond. Uncomfortable situations need not
always be bad situations. It will be just as important for you to
know how to react in a stressful but positive scenario.

By giving some time to thinking about what you would do and
how you would do it, you start the process of making positive
lifestyle changes. It will help you to take stock of your current
situation and review what kind of person you really want to be.
Do you feel negative about yourself? Are you prepared to
continue to allow yourself to feel negative about yourself? How
do you currently deal with those negative feelings? If you store
them away, basically ignoring them, you have a recipe for
disaster.

This process is not merely limited to a reality check of your
feelings. Carrying out this process facilitates effective changes to
your beliefs, attitudes and behaviours. Now you will find that
any change you make is not just a change for the sake of a
change, but it has a direction and a focus on something more
positive and productive in your life.

Acting assertively will allow you to feel self-confident and this
will generally gain the respect of your peers and friends. Low
self-esteem and lack of assertiveness come from a common core.
Generally they are associated with the assumptions we make
about how others see us, how we see them and how we
communicate and interact with each other. Socially, we set
boundaries for particular behaviours, be it our own or others'.
We learn what acceptable behaviour is from others as well as
from responses to our own actions and often these two are very
different. We set spatial boundaries based upon experiences, and
if a person has had a series of bad experiences then this can lead
to a negative change in the way they perceive themselves, the
way they behave, and their attitude towards others in similar
situations.

Learning to be more assertive

When you don't believe you have rights it is possible to react passively to circumstances and events in your life. If you allow the needs, opinions and judgements of others to become more important than your own, it is likely you'll feel hurt, anxious and even angry. This kind of passive or non-assertive behaviour is often indirect, emotionally dishonest and, ultimately, self-denying. This stems from what is essentially a position of ignorance, not because you are an ignorant person but because you did not make the effort to find out or know something about your rights. Assertive people know their rights and respect the rights of others.

Specific techniques for assertiveness skills

Here are some valuable and positive steps to take to develop your assertiveness. Use the following statements to announce what you want, think and feel with clarity:

- *I want to...*
- *I don't want you to...*
- *Would you...?*
- *I liked it when you did that.*
- *I have a different opinion. I think that...*
- *I have mixed feeling about this. I agree with these aspects for these reasons, but I am concerned about these aspects for these reasons.* It will be helpful to explain exactly what you mean and exactly what you don't mean, such as *I don't want to leave the company over this, but I'd like to talk it through and see if we can prevent it from happening again.*

Be direct! Deliver your message to the person for whom it is intended. If you want to **tell** Bill something, tell Bill, not everyone except Bill. Don't tell a group of which Bill is a member just so that Bill will get to know. Talk with him directly. Own your message! Acknowledge that your message is your view, your idea of good versus bad or right versus wrong, your beliefs. You can acknowledge ownership with personalized statements such as *I don't agree with you* (as opposed to *No, you're wrong*) or *I'd like you to feed the dog* (as opposed to *Hey! You really should feed the dog, you know*). Ask for feedback: *Am I making myself clear to you? How do you see this situation? What do you want to do?* Asking for feedback can encourage others to correct any misperceptions and help them realize that you are expressing an opinion, feeling or desire rather than a demand. Encourage others to be clear, direct and specific in their feedback to you.

Summary

It is important to us all to have the courage and skills to stand up for what we believe is right. Whether we decide to do so at any given time is another matter. You must use good judgement. People will without doubt judge you on what you say and do, the way you say it and the way in which you do it. Their overall judgement is irrespective of your understanding or intent and if you care about the way you are perceived by them then you will certainly be interested in making the right changes to ensure they don't judge you wrongly. Acting aggressively will have you pigeonholed as an aggressive individual when you might not be. It might well have been the case that at that moment you were simply reacting in an aggressive manner as a coping strategy, as opposed to being intrinsically an aggressive person. The important thing is not whether you are or are not an aggressive person but how you behave towards others, particularly in a hostile situation. An aggressive act can easily be interpreted as a challenge, a tendency that can have dire consequences in a hostile situation. It is generally best to wait and channel any aggression you have to when you need it most. Acting assertively will help you gain the respect of others, which in turn should help your confidence.

Be clear in what you say and if you have any doubts, say it over in your head first **before engaging your mouth.**

02 conflict and anger management

In this chapter you will learn:
- how conflicts arise and how to manage them
- the effects of anger and how to manage this sensation
- how to resolve problems.

Conflict

Some issues are very emotive and sometimes you can feel your anger building from within ready to make you explode. Conflicts occur when differences of opinion escalate into argument and contradictory (even violent) behaviour. At the heart of a conflict may be a disagreement about working conditions, or idle gossip, a threat, etc. It will likely cause us to act in an unusual way. We can all feel, in the heat of the moment, a sense that we are right and the world around us has gone crazy. This should ring alarm bells in your head. Pause to raise the question: *Am I thinking this through rationally?*

The way people behave towards each other is a very complex science which doesn't always bring about the intended result. This book seeks to give you advice on how to raise your own personal awareness and help you make the right decisions when faced with a conflict. The rest, as they say, is up to you.

Asserting yourself will not necessarily guarantee you happiness or fair treatment from others, neither will it solve all your personal problems or guarantee that others will be assertive and not aggressive towards you. Just because you assert yourself does not mean you will always get what you want. However, lack of assertiveness is most certainly one of the reasons why conflicts occur in relationships.

One useful approach to avoiding conflicts or arguments is effectively to **mind your own business**. A great many people would agree that it is very irritating to have someone butt in halfway through a discussion or an argument and muddy the waters. Having your opinion is a valuable asset but it is not always necessary to voice it. Try to do so only when invited to. Learning to use good judgement about whether to state your opinion is an extremely valuable skill. Don't be drawn into an argument; simply agree to disagree.

Another useful method to use is to state that you don't have a view on a particular aspect, even if you do. This is called **sitting on the fence** and effectively denies support to any side of an argument, thereby defusing your involvement. While this is a useful strategy, I would not suggest you use it all the time. There will be occasions when you need to express your opinion and state what you feel or believe. This will be a judgement call for you, and your decision should be based on a balanced consideration of keeping quiet or saying your piece.

Many people hide their intentions behind clever words and may have an agenda different from yours. This agenda could involve usurping your position or trying to make use of your good character to make them appear better than they really are. If this is a regular occurrence then perhaps you might examine why others are looking for conflict with you. This is not always clear. Sometimes people take advantage because they can or because you allow it. Building bridges between people is far more beneficial. Learn as much as you can about a person and you may find that they have similar if not identical views to you. We are all more the same than we are unique. Exude a friendly disposition and you will attract the same.

Conflict management

Conflict management means finding resolutions to interpersonal problems. While our society debates and apparently extols a zero tolerance approach to anti-social behaviour, it is more than a little naive to believe that this ideal can be fully implemented. We are all human, after all. When people are thrust together to coexist in a relatively small place there will inevitably be disagreements on various topics and of various magnitudes. That being the case, it is important that each of us knows what we can do if and when any conflict arises. Recognizing these differences and respecting the views of others can defuse a potentially violent encounter. After all, we don't all have to be the same or agree with each other.

From an individual perspective there are mechanisms you can employ to resolve conflicts. You might wish to figure out what it is that is actually making you angry or frustrated. Talk to someone you trust about your feelings to gauge whether you are being overly sensitive, fearful or anxious. If a conflict is tending towards violent behaviour then reject taunts for a fight and try to find a compromise instead. Avoid being enticed to some place where you will be alone. Avoid being in places in which conflicts can arise – **seek people**.

Decide on how you want to handle a situation and just do it. This can mean getting someone else to resolve the dispute (e.g. a mediator), walking away, talking the problem out calmly, avoiding certain people, etc. Honest communication which is self-enhancing and expressive can increase your chances for honest relationships and help you to feel better about yourself and your self-control in everyday situations.

Managing a conflict between people can be very difficult, particularly when emotions and tempers are running high and aggressive behaviour is expressed. Here is a series of steps to take to ensure that a resolution is reached:

1 **Ground rules.** It will be important to identify the need for all parties to work together, and an agreement that the parties involved share this need is a good starting point. Setting ground rules will essentially facilitate any debate or arguments in an appropriate way. It should be made clear that no one should revert to name calling, blaming, shouting, yelling or persistent interrupting. These factors all lead to chaos and prevent any resolution being arrived at.

2 **Listening.** It will be essential that the parties involved listen to each other and use sensitivity to ensure that their case is heard. The important factor here is to understand what someone wants and why. Only by keeping calm and listening actively can this be achieved.

3 **Common ground.** It will be useful to assert what the facts are and what aspects of any conflict or dispute are agreed on, and by carrying out the process it will lead to the determination of what is important to each party.

4 **Brainstorming.** Encourage all parties to list ideas or options without any feeling that they must be carried out. Having done that, this step will include thinking about solutions in which everyone gains something.

5 **Discussion.** During this step, each person's view of a proposed solution should be discussed to try to reach an acceptable compromise for everyone involved.

6 **Record.** It will be important to make an accurate record of what was agreed and each person be allowed to state their interpretation of it. This will be a useful reference should the conflict arise again in the future.

These steps can be carried out in any situation almost anywhere.

Anger

Anger is an emotion that everybody feels and expresses. It is a natural human emotion that must be managed effectively otherwise it can become the source of physical, mental, emotional, social and legal problems. Common means of expressing anger include venting, seeking revenge and expressing dislike. Most people suffering anger avoid seeking help because they do not perceive they have a problem. It can be very useful to learn how to channel your aggression or anger positively.

Anger is normally expressed as two main types: a purposeful type and a spontaneous type. They both relate to intention to hurt or cause damage. Purposeful anger has a high degree of premeditation or thoughtful planning and is delivered with a high degree of self-control. This version can be very much a vengeful or retaliatory type. Spontaneous anger is immediate, has little premeditation and is delivered with little to moderate self-control. This version is like a firework, a big explosion that doesn't last very long. The two types of anger happen at different times. The spontaneous type occurs immediately after the fact, whereas the purposeful type occurs later.

In terms of usefulness, the expression of anger can be constructive or destructive. Constructive anger expression mirrors assertive behaviour and is a realization and acknowledgement of our personal boundaries without threatening someone else's. Constructive anger includes, for example, channelling anger and aggressive energies through a sport to produce something more positive. Destructive expression, by contrast, is never productive, although it can be defensive. Through destructive anger we defensively protect vulnerable identities, retaliate with hostility or violence, and deny ourselves the possibility of expressing our angry feelings in any other way. This could lead to the suffering of psychological problems. These distinctions are depicted in Table 2.1 and are summarized as:

- Purposeful constructive expression involves assertiveness and productive behaviours.
- Purposeful destructive expression leads to hostility.
- Spontaneous constructive expression leads to passion and suffering.
- Spontaneous destructive expression leads to rage, violence, screaming and striking out.

	Purposeful	**Spontaneous**
Constructive	Assertiveness	Passion and suffering
Destructive	Hostility	Rage, violence, screaming and striking out

table 2.1 defining expressions of anger

What causes us to become angry? Someone insults you by calling you an *inconsiderate idiot* and it may make you feel irate or angry. Perhaps another driver cuts in front of you while you're driving, causing you to feel anger. Maybe you have read an article depicting unnecessary hardship or torture to a creature or another human and you feel angry. These feelings of anger share a common relationship. They are infringements that affect the values by which we live and make us perceive a loss of control over factors that affect those values. Those values may be love, devotion, pride or fairness, etc. Anger stems from fear and a sense of helplessness and can be sensed as a perceived threat to our beliefs. We can also sense anger if a frustration is not resolved. Anger is a basic human trait and subconsciously we use it as a defence mechanism when a conflict cannot be resolved. It can make us believe that lashing out (a burst of physical energy at a perceived threat) will defeat our opposition or break the barrier stopping us from reaching our goal – which is generally safety or the resolution of the conflict. In this way, anger can be used constructively to provide us with the energy to fight back when we need it. Yet anger mostly clouds our ability to make proper judgements and creates extra stress. This is the start of a self perpetuating cycle.

Anger management

Identifying the cause will be a major step towards eliminating or understanding what makes you angry. In order to reduce your anger to a controllable level, think carefully about the following.

Develop empathetic understanding

Blaming 'others' for a given situation and directing your anger at 'them' can seem a natrual path at times. Stop! If you begin to feel angry with someone ask them to explain their point of view. Encourage them to talk about their underlying beliefs or background views that lead to their point of view. Understanding their point of view will help you become empathetic.

Accept reality and forgive

Some anger may stem from a belief that others have unfairly received more than we have, leading to resentment. It is important to understand that the resentment you experience is sourced by jealousy and vanity. These are strong destructive emotions and only understanding and forgiveness can resolve these feelings.

Examine your expectations

It is all too easy to become angry at yourself or others when things don't go according to plans or expectations. Life is always ready to serve a curve ball and throw your well-laid plans into chaos. It's how you deal with those events that determine your resolve. The key is to set only achievable (albeit challenging!) expectations for yourself. By doing this you can make modifications to what you do to reach your expectation or goal.

Make a blame list

Many psychologists recommend this method. If you are holding on to some event or episode in your life which has caused you great pain or feelings of hurt, or you associate those feelings to a particular person, you may want to punish this person. You may think that you are punishing them by holding on to the feeling associated by this event, but holding on to the anger is only hurting *you*. Make a list of all those whom you wish to blame. Try to see things from their perspective and accept the reality of the situation.

Happiness or anger

Holding on to anger has destructive consequences, including negative physiological effects to your body. You cannot feel happy and angry at the same time – it is impossible. You have a very basic choice: either feel angry or feel happy.

Meditation

Finding a way to relax and focus your thoughts will be an extremely useful step in developing an overall plan to deal with your anger. Concentrate on one or more situations where you become angry and mentally role play (visualize) overcoming your anger in that situation. Develop your own list of things to say to yourself whenever you feel angry. Use positive self-talk to reassure yourself.

Time out

When people become angry, more often than not they behave in an irrational and abnormal way. On reflection, those who have been angry can feel either vindicated or guilty about their actions. In dealing with people who are behaving so, it is a good tactic to use a timeout device: this is a period of time during which all parties are separated, can cool down and return to their 'normal' calm demeanour.

Wouldn't it be better if someone known to you, whom you like, tells you that they care about you but is angry over something you did or said? Would it not be more constructive if this person were to take time to listen to your point of view and work on solutions to the problem? Honesty starts by recognition and acceptance that there is a solution to your anger problem. Remember, anger only hurts *you*. Finally, you might find these two suggestions useful for recognizing how your anger can be resolved:

1 Make a list of your self-destructive expressions of anger – this involves listing ways in which you deal with frustrating situations, thoughts that increase your anger, feelings you experience if you internalize anger (often known as bottling it up), words or actions you use that are harmful to others, your relationships and yourself. Then consider what thoughts and actions would be more constructive in each case and replace the destructive ones.

   Make a list of energetic activities to reduce your anger arousal. What helps you reduce the feelings that arouse you to anger? Consider taking up a sport, such as cycling, swimming, walking, running, or doing household or garden chores. What about talking and laughing?

2 Develop a plan for assertive conflict management. In particular, consider how to deal assertively with situations in which you tend to be angry and aggressive. Seek win–win solutions where the compromise on each side is equal and leads to resolution.

Summary

There is no path in life that has no conflicts. It is how we deal with those conflicts that reflect who we are. Having a self-determined and single-minded approach to life and our personal safety seems to be one of the keys. As a famous teacher once told me: *There are two paths in life, but for all those who ever arrived, there was only one.* If you bind anger and aggression together you have a very unstable recipe. Don't accept that, either from others or from yourself.

03 communication skills

In this chapter you will learn:
- the difference between verbal and nonverbal communications
- how to become a good communicator
- how to interpret nonverbal signs, signals and gestures.

Communication skills can be beneficial in every aspect of our lives. The way you communicate with others determines your success, be it in business, social scenarios or simply on an interpersonal level. Learning what to say and how to say it can get you out of a potentially dangerous situation. Talking your way out of a situation is far better than fighting your way out. While there can be no catalogue of what to say in any given situation, this chapter will help you determine what changes you can make to improve the way you communicate.

It is hard to conceive how man coped in the preverbal ages, when language was nothing more than grunts and interpretation of body language, yet clearly he did. Communication in this modern world has changed radically in the last 100 years or so with technological advancements appearing ever more rapidly. Transportation has made sending of mail more efficient, the telephone and television have facilitated greater contact between people and the Internet has taken communication to a completely new level. A mere century ago these inventions were considered fanciful ideas, but now they are so much part of our daily lives that many of us would now feel lost without them.

This part of the book deals with the way we communicate and how we interpret the communications of others. You will need to understand and take stock of your current communication methods before going on to change and improve your techniques.

Communication skills comprise two parts: verbal and nonverbal skills (Table 3.1). Verbal skills are subdivided further into talking and listening. Nonverbal skills include body language and other signs and signals. Both categories effectively send messages between individuals.

Verbal Communications	Non Verbal Communications (NVC)
Talking Listening	Body language Other signs and signals

table 3.1 components of communication skills

Verbal and nonverbal communications are very different in both their content and form: put simply, the former is audibly based and the latter visually based. Together they can present a powerful message – but get it wrong and conflicts in communication arise, resulting in a recipe for trouble.

Talking

Language is one of the most powerful tools we have for conveying messages, including, unfortunately, ones we may not have intended. In difficult or awkward situations we all use phrases, words, clichés and axioms to pad out what we are saying rather than getting to the point. This is not the most effective use of language and signifies that the person talking is searching for the right words or perhaps has not thought the whole matter through. Verbal messages are usually high in content or information and in many cases give too much information to be digested or assimilated in one go. In the early 1980s the national coaching foundation carried out a study to determine how much information people gain from the spoken word. The results, amazingly, showed that the actual amount of information gleaned is very little but that the spoken word, when underpinned with other factors, completes the picture. Table 3.2 represents these results.

The words that are used	7%
The way in which they are said	38%
The way the speaker behaves	55%

table 3.2 breakdown of the spoken word

Do not fall into the trap of thinking that content is unimportant. **What** you say underpins the other elements. Nevertheless, you must use words in the correct way to get your point across. Do not beat around the bush. Focus on what you really want to say and say it. Keep your words high on information and low on waffle.

The way we behave while delivering the message adds colour to enhance our words. This is normally known as the **form** of the communication, which can be further subdivided into voice quality, or paralanguage.

Voice quality/paralanguage

The quality of your voice can indicate many things. It can announce what kind of mood you are in and whether you are being sincere or not. The quality of your voice will make what you say either interesting or boring, not because the content itself is boring but because your voice is more or less easy to listen to. A high-pitched voice may indicate feelings of joy, fear or anger. A low-pitched voice may indicate tiredness, calmness or depression. Someone who speaks fast is likely to be excited, anxious or insecure whereas someone who speaks slowly exudes sincerity, confidence or thoughtfulness. The use of a loud voice indicates confidence, enthusiasm or aggression and a soft voice usually indicates trust, caring or understanding. There is a great deal of evidence that children in primary school are more receptive to a soft and caring, perhaps almost maternal, voice. Despite growing older and maturing we never really lose the need to hear a nurturing voice. This can be very useful when attempting to soothe a person who is angry or outwardly aggressive (see Chapter 02).

Paralanguage refers to four main elements that essentially affect the quality of our voice and make it interesting. Components of paralanguage are:

- pitch – high or low
- resonance – rich or thin
- tempo – fast or slow, rhythmical or monotone
- volume – loud or quiet.

Learning to control these qualities will enrich your voice and make it more compelling and easier to listen to. Moreover, it provides you with a distinct advantage when dealing with situations you might find hostile or uncomfortable. Making good use of your voice is a constructive element not just in self defence but also in all aspects of your life.

Positive self-talk

This is a very interesting aspect of talking, because it does not involve communication with anyone else. It involves **you talking to yourself**, whether that be inside your head or actually verbalizing it, almost like a mantra. Psychologists have been aware of the effects of self-talk for many years. Sportsmen and women have used this as a form of confidence building for motivation and verbal self-support. In contrast, many people who worry or are anxious about what they are doing often develop a self-destroying syndrome with negative self-talk.

Positive self-talk is a very worthwhile tool to help encourage anyone to do the things they most want to do. Telling yourself that you 'can do it' is a form of positive self-talk. This is a tool you can teach yourself and it involves you talking to yourself in an encouraging or motivating way. Telling yourself: *Keep calm, I know I can do this*, in a potentially hostile situation when tempers are becoming frayed will help you keep control of your behaviour. Remember, you can only be directly responsible for what you do, not the actions of others. It can also be useful in situations when adrenalin is rushing into your stomach (the sensation of 'butterflies') and making you feel very nervous.

Practise to begin with by looking at yourself in a mirror. Listen to the positive message of what you are saying (whether out loud or in your head) and remember how it makes you feel. Learning to associate the words with feeling confident, motivated and encouraged will be key to success. Everyone does this at some stage of their everyday lives, whether it's debating to buy one pair of shoes over another, a magazine or save the money. Learning to recognize it as a skill you can focus on is a valuable step to make and one I would heartily recommend.

Listening

This is a skill that involves using both eyes and ears and facilitates the bridging between verbal and nonverbal communications. It's not one many of us are good at but it certainly is extremely important in communication. The eyes will determine the nonverbal language and the ears the audible message. Together they allow us to interpret what has been said and the way in which it has been delivered. How often do you fall into the trap of interpreting what you've heard, or plan a response, while a person is still talking to you? This process is often referred to as thinking on your feet. We are all guilty of this and it will affect your ability to communicate efficiently.

You need to listen carefully first, then respond. Listening relies on being attentive, which means looking at the speaker and paying attention to what is being said. It also relies on active listening, which means not interrupting and speaking over the top of someone else and encouraging them to speak using bridging techniques. Being attentive and listening actively makes the speaker feel respected and that their ideas are understood. So by listening, interaction between two people, i.e. the speaker and you, becomes more meaningful.

Good communicators try to separate fact from fiction and are willing to share the needs and expectations of others. Are you a good communicator? Good listening skills means:

- concentration on the speaker
- listening with openness
- listening to the content
- recognizing that it is a very important skill
- listening with empathy
- listening actively.

Keeping things moving

There are techniques you can use to keep a conversation going back and forwards or just one way for that matter. These are particularly useful for seeking clarification of what the speaker has just said or to reinforce understanding. Such techniques are commonplace, are very useful, can be utilized as effective listening skills and include the following:

- **Being attentive.** Look and listen. Make eye contact and do not pre-empt what is being said.
- **Avoiding interruption.** Allow the speaker to say their piece. Ask questions and allow an answer.
- **Paraphrasing.** This is repeating what the speaker has said in a different way to show you wish clarity or that you understand what has been said.
- **Bridging.** These are techniques used to encourage the speaker to continue by acknowledging intermittently: *I see, Yes, OK,* etc. Bridging reinforces your respect for the speaker.

As a listener, these skills are particularly useful and encourage the speaker to continue.

A breakdown in communications is generally the most common cause of disagreements or conflicts. This is a phenomenon that occurs daily, so how does this happen? Common causes are shown in Table 3.3. Breakdown is essentially caused either by the person sending the message inappropriately or by the person receiving the message inappropriately. In the top part of Table 3.3 you will see that the sender can cause a breakdown if their message is wrong or if it contains inappropriate information. Consider this situation: John wants to alert the fire authorities to attend to No. 35 Main Street where he sees smoke coming from the front window of the house which has a brown door. John tells the emergency operator: *Go to No. 53. It has a dark coloured door.* In this instance John has given wrong information because he became flustered in the heat of the moment and did not focus on delivering the correct information. In another version of the same event, John tells the operator: *The house at No. 35 with the white painted bay windows with green and red striped curtains, red front door with a brass letterbox, stone lion dogs in the garden next to the lily pond in which the owner, who is a really nice gentleman of about 55 years old who always shops at the local 24-hour corner shop because he doesn't like crowds, placed a replica crane to stop the birds from eating his koi carp. Oh, and I think it might be on fire.* Now John's message is full of irrelevant information.

Causes of communication breakdown	

1 **Sending messages**	• The content is:
	  – wrong, inappropriate or incorrect
	  – too complicated
	  – too long
	  – given at the wrong time
	• Inconsistent or mixed messages. There is a conflict between what is said and how it is said (non verbal communication)
	• The form of the message is inappropriate, e.g. *I didn't mean to say it like that*

2 **Receiving messages**	• Receiver is not listening or attending to what is said • Receiver misinterprets content or form

table 3.3 breakdown in communications

The lower part of Table 3.3 shows that the person receiving the message can cause the breakdown, either by missing the message because they were not listening, or by misinterpreting the content or the form. The receiver must be ready to accept the message and be able to interpret the message as it was designed, otherwise a breakdown will happen.

Qualities of a good communicator

1 They continually set explicit and verifiable outcomes and goals.
2 They have sensory awareness and observational skills to provide them with feedback about their progress towards their outcomes.
3 They have flexibility of behaviour and continually change and adjust their communications to achieve the outcomes. If one approach isn't working they have the flexibility to easily switch to another.

How to say *no* and mean it

NO is not a dirty word! Do you currently say yes just to avoid hurting someone's feelings or because you don't want to explain why you want to say no? My research has shown that some girls on a night out may kiss a persistent male just to get rid of him. This action is dangerous and sends out the wrong message. It is more likely to encourage rather than dissuade and is more likely to build expectations than make your point. Learning how to say no is important and will rely on increasing your self-respect; your confidence in your decision making; and understanding that your worth does not depend on other people's judgements. Remember, you simply cannot please all the people all the time.

Here are some excellent steps to take when developing the ability to say no. Practise each in turn and your confidence will grow every time you make a successful step.

1 **Selection.** First, pick a situation in which you inappropriately said yes when you would rather have said no.
2 **Identify reasons.** Ask yourself why you said yes. What were the reasons? Were you worried that you might damage your relationship with that person, offend them or hurt their feelings?
3 **Prevention.** Plan to avoid putting yourself in the same situation and, if unavoidable, plan a new response.
4 **Role play.** Practise your new response. Listen to how you sound and feel when you say no. Watch yourself in a mirror and see how others see you. Try to do it skilfully and firmly without being provocative. Select a good uninvolved friend to help you rehearse this and elicit their feedback as to your progress. Depending on the feedback, you can make changes to your voice and body language to ensure that your message is delivered properly.

Before you agree to anything, be sure that you really want to do it. Action other than this will only make you feel even guiltier. Don't cave in just because of someone else's feelings. Your feelings are more important. You have to live with yourself and not anyone else's feelings. Don't feel compelled to say yes to return a friend's favour either. A true friend will understand if you cannot genuinely return a favour.

Making the problem worse

There are many ways in which you can make a problem worse. Some of these can be lifestyle issues but, generally speaking, behaviours and body language are the culprits:

- **A sharp retort.** If you encounter youthful hostility, and some youths can be foul mouthed, it's very easy to deliver a one-liner in order to shut them up. However, this is only likely to exacerbate matters further and make you even angrier.
- **Becoming defensive.** It is very easy to become defensive if someone suggests that you shoulder some blame for something you are not responsible for. Whether you are responsible or not, defaulting to defensive posturing can make things volatile. Others will continue to load blame as you deny all responsibility. This is a conflict which can be difficult to resolve quickly. However you can learn methods to state your case without becoming defensive and perhaps redirect blame to someone else, such as the person who is actually responsible.
- **Avoiding the issue.** As a factor responsible for communication breakdown, ignoring an issue by not attending to it can cause friction. Likewise, deliberately avoiding talking about an issue by cleverly manipulating conversation is equally irritating.
- **Taking the matter personally.** Taking things to heart is a self-destructive habit and can result in making you feel guilty or, indeed, cause behaviours that would make others behave negatively towards you.

These are all counterproductive responses and reduce the chance of transforming a negative encounter to a constructive one. They diminish any control you might exercise in order to calm a situation by using positive behaviours.

Telling a lie and feeling good about it

In a violent or hostile situation telling a lie to protect yourself is nothing more than a tactic of deception. Creating a pseudo-character or telling a few white lies to protect your feelings in this situation is not a crime. Nothing will be lost, neither your integrity nor your honesty (see Rule 4 in Chapter 05). This may go as far as telling the other person just what they want to hear or telling a blatant lie. Telling a lie is a coping mechanism when one is placed in a state of fear. Fear is the underlying motivation and while deception is the intent there will be little concern for long-term effects, if, indeed, there are any. We learn how to lie in childhood and by the time we are mature the ability to lie has become more sophisticated. The objective is not to feel good about telling lies per se but you should not feel guilty when you have to tell a lie to protect yourself in the instance of danger.

Jane was trapped between two good-looking guys during a night out with the girls. She knew by the tone of the conversation directed at her that their interest in her was more intimate than she cared for. She didn't want to leave the party or her friends so Jane devised a pseudo-character called Pamela who had no liking for boys but more of a penchant for older women. She then moved away from the guys to sit with an older female friend. Jane made use of telling a lie to defuse a situation she felt uncomfortable in. No harm done.

Derek had just left the office and stepped into the street when he was accosted by two mean-looking men. They asked him for his wallet and while it was still in his pocket he explained that he had left it in his desk. He also explained that four other executives were just leaving the office behind him and that they would surely be caught. The two took to their heels. There were no other executives following him, but placing the idea of fear in their minds helped Derek escape.

Touch

This tactile form of communication is a very intimate activity and may sometimes be culturally based. Those from Mediterranean countries such as Spain and Italy are known for hugging, kissing and touching. This is all totally acceptable in their culture but outside it may cause offence. British people are considered a bit straightlaced and often back away from this form of familiarity. The biggest problem with touch is its interpretation: much depends on how you perceive it. It can be very intimate, or have a calming effect if a person is already upset, or quite the reverse. Any kind of touching, from an embrace, to stroking the hand or placing a hand on the arm or around the shoulder, can be interpreted differently subject to the situation. The action may be the same but the message is clearly very different.

There are many situations in which we allow touch because it's expected: in hospital, or when you visit the local sports clinic, during congratulatory occasions, etc. There are other situations where touch is rightly frowned on, for instance when working with children, or perhaps in the office. Consider the scenario: if a man deliberately presses himself up against a woman in a confined space, for example on a busy train or in a lift, he might be hoping that she will assume it isn't his fault and therefore not react in a negative way. An innocent man would not do this to a woman and he would do whatever he could to prevent it. The best way to deal with this type of scenario is:

1 to move away
2 to say something loudly or attract attention to him causing embarrassment
3 if it persists you would be within your right to hit back physically; however, it's up to you to decide what is right in this situation.

Flirtation

Flirting is a proverbial minefield because it can send out all the wrong messages. Alan Sugar, the business tycoon, believes there is no place for this form of communication in the workplace. Certainly flirting can redirect attentions and motivations away from those required to see a task completed. It can also negatively affect the relationships between workers and colleagues. If you think flirting is an acceptable business tactic, think again.

In fact, flirting happens everywhere people congregate. It's not just a realm of the workplace. It can be a smile, a suggestive look, the use of innuendo in conversation. The list is endless. Flirting is a social expression between people, an activity that either sex can participate in without becoming actually physically involved.

Flirting is also a preamble to establishing a sexual relationship – and here's where the problems start. Consider this: you suddenly realize you have put yourself in a stupid situation (most people have done it at some stage of their lives). You need to acknowledge that when you know you've done something stupid or sent the wrong signals, it isn't too late to back out or to stop the situation getting worse. Have a plan or mechanism ready for such an occasion. Make an excuse to leave or simply apologize that you have to be somewhere else. The clear advice is: if you don't want to tango, don't get up to dance. The danger is if you make the opportunity available, the wrong person might just take it. This can put you in a very invidious situation indeed. The choice, however, is yours!

There is a very fine line between flirting and sexual harassment. Sexual harassment was brought into law in 1980 under the Sex Discrimination Act 1975. It criminalizes a range of actions from indecent or suggestive remarks to unwelcome behaviour of a sexual nature, including demands for sex for advancement or promotion or by blackmail. It includes the hanging of any pornographic material, for example a calendar depicting nudity, in public view. Either sex ought to have more respect for each other in all aspects of their social interaction and avoid bringing this type of expression into being.

Nonverbal communications

As you become more assertive, remember to use your assertiveness skills selectively. It is not just what you say to someone verbally, but also how you communicate nonverbally, with your voice tone, gesture, eye contact, facial expression, posture and dress that will influence your impact on others. You must remember that it takes time and practice, as well as a willingness to accept yourself as you make mistakes, to reach the goal of acting assertively. People who understand and care about you are your strongest assets and they will provide you with the information about how you conduct yourself. This information will be necessary for you to recognize the need for change and to make changes.

Nonverbal communication incorporates many forms, including signs, gestures, body language, the written word, photographs, silent movies – the list goes on. In this modern world we are bombarded with nonverbal communication in every minute of our daily lives. Walking down the high street you will see signs shouting SALE! to lure you in to buy, signs to direct to the biggest bargains, posters and videos depicting models posing or modelling garments or products, all inducing you to buy. However compelling these signs are, we ultimately have the decision to act on them or not. Not all the signs and signals that dominate our life are driven by the marketing gurus. During the same walk down the high street you will observe traffic regulation signs, public information signs such as street names, directions, maps, etc. These signs can be very powerful and so too can 'body language'. The way we conduct ourselves reveals more than we bargain for. Body language works on all your senses, but most commonly on sight. The most obvious form is facial expression because whenever you speak, others look at your face.

Try this experiment. Sit in front of a mirror and make an angry scowl while saying in a very happy and light voice that you're having a nice day. Your expression tends to set the tone of the scene that lies ahead and it will be very noticeable just how confusing the message is. Making sure that your face portrays the right message in a self defence situation will be important to you. You should practise looking confident but not afraid, even though you may feel afraid. Being assertive in this type of instance most certainly gives you an edge.

Body language

Interpreting body language in isolation can be a very dangerous road to travel and it is more likely than not that you'll get it wrong. This type of communication must be observed and assimilated alongside other forms such as talking, information or content and form. Let's just consider how you stand and how the message can be interpreted. For this purpose look at the four illustrations opposite.

Figure 3.1 – a shrug of the shoulders can imply a whole host of things such as disinterest, being resigned to something, doubt or blatant disregard of something.

Figure 3.2 – leaning against a wall with a hand on the hip can imply relaxing, casuality, impatience, someone who is self-satisfied or someone who is becoming angry. The posture in Figure 3.3 can indicate shyness, self-consciousness, coyness, modesty, shame, guilt or sadness. Notice that the head is tilted down showing a form of recessive behaviour. The last example,

Figure 3.4, can represent surprise, aloofness, domination, suspicion or indecision. The upright position, arms folded and feet spread, indicates a very confident or defiant person, or someone who wants to be dominant. The slight tilt of the upper torso away from the subject is indicative of doubting or disbelief.

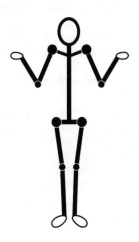

figure 3.1 a shrug

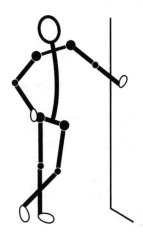

figure 3.2 leaning against a wall, hand on hip

figure 3.3 posture indicating recessive behaviour

figure 3.4 upright position, tilting torso

These postural messages give us additional information about the person we are looking at. Table 3.4 shows us further examples of body language.

Gestures	Clapping, shaking hands, nodding head, clenching fists, etc.
Posture	This indicates attitude, for example: • standing upright – power, assertiveness, respect • slumping – disinterest or relaxation • seated but leaning forwards – aggression or interest • walking – from wild enthusiasm to boredom
Body contact	Kissing, shaking hands, back patting, poking, punching, slapping, etc.
Spatial awareness	The distance between two people can change the meaning of the message, for example saying something directly to a person while standing behind them can change the intent
Clothes	A clean, smart appropriately dressed person will command respect
Appearance	Good appearance (i.e. good posture, good clothes and appropriate gestures) encourages others to have confidence in you

table 3.4 examples of nonverbal communication

What does it all mean?

It is very difficult to make generalizations on the interpretation of any singular action of body language because, like words, every action must be considered in context. Consider this: standing with your arms folded and leaning against a wall could mean that you are lazy, arrogant, disinterested, fed up or simply relaxing and waiting for something. Picking the wrong 'meaning' could cause you to jump to the wrong conclusion.

Psychologists have written a great many books and spent many years researching the meaning of various gestures. The same gesture in different situations carries a different meaning. An example of this is giving the two-finger gesture (or V sign). Churchill used it to indicate victory in World War 2. English archers used it at the Battle of Agincourt to sneer at their French opponents to say *I still have mine*. (Captured English archers had their first two fingers cut off by the French to prevent them from shooting their arrows at them.) Nowadays this gesture has a hostile and derogatory meaning. You can see now how the same action carried out in three different situations can mean three different things.

Cultural contexts are also relevant. What is acceptable in one culture may be offensive in another. Remember that someone from another culture may display offensive behaviour without having any intention to offend. Of course this doesn't excuse blatant behaviour which is without doubt offensive. In instances such as this it might be prudent just to point out that they are behaving in an offensive manner. They may be shocked at this and apologize or you may well find out that their intent was simply deliberately well hidden.

So with all these variables, how can you know just what a person is telling you? In the end it just comes down to practice. Observe the world around you. You will see from the many examples you witness every day that body language is a helpful way to understand what a person really wants to tell you but doesn't. But it is far from being an exact science. This is why verbal communication is the only way to confirm and clarify interpretation. If you send the wrong signals you could just be making the matter worse and placing yourself in danger.

How it all works

Something said is misconstrued; a supportive gesture is misinterpreted. It doesn't take much to raise a person's hackles. Just remember that there is without doubt a correct way to conduct yourself in every situation, whether that be at work, play or at home, and generally this involves having and giving respect for everyone. Strangely enough, we are all conditioning one another to place a bias on the negative qualities of our behaviours. Once a negative act is identified we respond in a way that brings a lot of attention to this act and yet whenever positive behaviour is perpetrated it is almost overlooked. Surely to bring a balance to our lives we need positively to reinforce good behaviours with encouraging words. The number of times

I have seen good, kind acts ignored by their recipients is staggering. The next time someone holds open a door for you, picks up your keys when you drop them or helps you out in any way, a simple word of thanks can go a long way to ensuring repeat behaviour.

If we continually look for the negative behaviours all we will ever **find** are negative behaviours. While it is right to recognize these behaviours it is wrong to believe that your life ought to be consumed searching for them. My wise old grandmother used to tell me: *Look for the good in people because trouble will come looking for you soon enough.* Never a truer word spoken. Being a respectful person will help you avoid causing offence and it will also help you become tolerable. After all, we all make mistakes of varying magnitudes and it is having the decency to be tolerant and respectful that will pave the way to your becoming a good person. Try to view a glance from others not as threatening, but perhaps as curious. You don't always have to make eye contact, as this in itself can be construed as confrontational. If you must look back, then smile. A smile can defuse many situations. You might also wish to engage the person in a very general conversation. People who stare at or admire you from a distance generally don't actually want to have any real interaction with you. They might have the desire within them but many never act on it.

Summary

The ability to communicate pervades all of life. In humans it can be as basic as movements of the body or the use of the eyes to convey our feelings. The spoken word permits us to engage in conversation or discourse on any subject. The words themselves are inept and, without context, can prove meaningless. Our body language (nonverbal communications) colours our words and helps increase the meaning and context of the verbal message. Messages are exchanges in a short space of time and it is vital we get it right. In self defence terms even a moment can appear to be a long time and it will be important to you to say the right thing at the right time. You should have all the tools and skills you need at the ready to keep you safe. Using communication skills will both help you convey the right messages as well as accurately interpret messages given to you.

Be alert, be safe.

04

being safe and secure

In this chapter you will learn:
- how to improve your home security
- how to increase your personal safety
- how to travel safely.

Many people consider their home to be their castle and believe it should be impregnable. However, the reality is there is no building an accomplished and determined burglar can't break into. Even HM Queen Elizabeth II has had more than one instance of unwanted visitation at Buckingham Palace. However, by following some simple steps you can make your house as safe as possible and, should anyone break into your home, make it difficult to go undetected.

Home security

The first important consideration of home safety is to have secure locks on all your doors and windows. The second most important is to **use them**.

Locks and keys

The most secure lock you can purchase is a five-lever deadbolt lock – the bolt fits squarely into the door jamb and cannot be dislodged with a plastic card or ruler or cut by a hacksaw. These locks can be purchased at any reputable locksmith or good DIY store. Fitting them may be tricky and an amateur approach may compromise the very security you are expecting from the locks. The best advice is to leave it to the experts. Never hide your keys in a so-called secret place, such as under the doormat or in a pot plant by the door etc.; burglars are well aware of this and can probably think of more places than you can. If you are afraid of being locked out give a key(s) to a neighbour or relative you trust. Whenever you move into a new flat or house, as a matter of course, have the locks changed, so former tenants or their friends will not have access to your belongings. Remember, some people do give out keys as a backup in case they lose theirs.

If your keys are lost or stolen report it to the police immediately and arrange to change the locks on your home at once. Most home insurance schemes cover this aspect (see following section on insurance). It is best not to have any form of identification on your keyring but if you feel you must, use an identification number such as the phone number of your insurance company or social security number. Don't ever use your postcode. It is also a good idea to keep your car keys on a separate ring from your house keys. That way if you lose your house keys at least your car can't be stolen.

When walking to your car, office or home, always have the appropriate key ready and in your hand. This will cut down the time spent in dark car parks and doorways fumbling about in handbags and pockets. Don't hide duplicate keys under the bonnet or bumper of your car – keep an extra set either at home or at your office or place of work (if it's safe and permitted). Remember, many car thieves check wheel arches and bumpers for spare keys.

Doors and windows

Almost every household door is hung on hinges, and making sure that the hinges are appropriate to the weight of the door provides the right kind of security. Hinges come in many forms depending on what the function of the door is: it could be a corridor door, a fire door, a multiuser entry door, etc. Security hinges not only function as a hinge but they have additional tungsten pins which locate into the door jamb making it nigh impossible to take the door off its hinges by force. The door frame is more likely to give way first.

Consider fitting the following to all external doors:

- Door viewer or spy hole to allow you to screen unwanted visitors.
- An intercom system to allow you to speak with callers at your house without allowing them in first.
- A door chain fitted between the door jamb and door is also advised. It will enable you to open the door a few inches to screen a person's credentials or identification. It can also be useful for receiving letters or small parcels.

Make sure you do this!

All windows in your home that are used for ventilation should be lockable. There are several methods to limit how far a window can be opened. With old-style sash windows, drive a large nail or a screw into the window sash at a point at which you want the window to stop when pushed up. Another method is to place a piece of wood such as a broomstick in the window runner, as this can allow you to regulate how far you want the window to open. Modern windows and double-glazed units usually come complete with Allen screw security locks fitted to the handles or the frame. They might also have alternative devices to prevent unwanted access so, if they are fitted, **please use them**. These windows usually have factory-fitted governors to limit how far they can open and have a safety release catch for opening wider. Familiarize yourself with how they work because this will be important if you ever need to escape via the window. Window burglar alarms can be purchased at all good DIY stores. They can be placed on any windows that are open for ventilation. They are triggered by movement so if someone tampers with the window the alarm will sound. These devices can be set so that small pets can enter and exit the house without triggering the alarm, but if a human tries it will set the alarm off.

Alarms and safes

If you keep large amounts of cash or other valuables at home or if you live in a high crime area, you should consider installing a burglar alarm in your home. There are many to choose from. One really effective model is a silent alarm, connected to a monitoring station. There are a number of companies available to install burglar alarms or, if you are adept at DIY, they can be fairly straightforward to install. As soon as anyone trips the alarm the signal sounds at the monitoring station and, in turn, the local police force is alerted, without the burglar being aware of having tripped the alarm. Better still, don't leave valuables at home; arrange for them to be kept secure at a bank deposit box or use a night safe for cash or business money. If you must keep valuables at home consider the installation of a floor safe. This is normally a very strong metal box installed to fit under and flush with the floor. It can be locked with a key, a combination code or remote keypad.

Don't forget about outhouses, such as sheds and garages that are not attached to the house. They too should be fitted with alarms or early warning devices alerting you to unwanted intrusion. They can also be hardwired to a house installation. Make sure your garage and front entrance are well lit. Fit floodlights to give you plenty of illumination when returning home at night and to deter intruders. There are a wide variety of lights which can be fitted to your house. These can be wired to operate with a passive infrared (PIR) detector which automatically switches the light on with any detected movement. These can also be triggered by heat and movement detection and can be adjusted to avoid causing annoyance to neighbours when a cat, hedgehog or other small animal breaks the infrared beam.

Insurance

Don't forget home insurance cover for all your valuables. There are many companies to choose from but please check that the cover extends to **all** your household needs and is sufficient. Over the years, many householders have purchased standard home insurance packages only to find the cover did not extend to lost items. Not every 'package' offered by insurance companies is the same and they all offer different cover. Ensure that you have cover for lost keys. With this, cover insurance companies arrange to have an accredited locksmith attend at your house, normally within an hour, to replace locks. It can be expensive to replace keys and locks if you lose your keys. In this instance it's a case of shopping around for the best deal and not forgetting to read the small print.

Feeling secure in your home

Keeping yourself safe while indoors is also important. Try to keep your curtains and blinds closed at night. This keeps passers-by and strangers from seeing you are alone, irrespective of whether you are or not, or otherwise studying your habits. To make it appear there are other people at home when you are alone, put the lights on in another room or turn a radio or TV on in another part of the house. If you hear suspicious noises pretend you are talking loudly to a partner or a spouse; also you may wish to consider calling the police.

You can purchase timer devices to attach to internal lights and these can be programmed to turn lights off or on as you choose, to give the illusion that someone is at home.

If you happen to live in a student residence, multistorey or high-rise building that has communal laundry rooms, try to co-ordinate your use of the laundry to coincide with a neighbour's – remember, there is safety in numbers. These places are targets for assailants and if you can't co-ordinate your times, **don't stay there alone**. Even if you have a key to lock yourself in, consider that you may be locking yourself in with an assailant. Better to put your washing on and lock it in and return for it later.

Domestic violence and abuse

Violence in the home or between relatives is known as domestic violence. Disturbingly family relationships can often be a source of physical violence or abuse whether it comes from a spouse, partner or another family member and whether the abuse is physical, sexual, psychological or emotional. It can often go on for many years, happening every once in a while or frequently, before a serious incident occurs or before the victim has the courage or the realization that it needs to be reported.

Domestic violence and abuse is an incredibly difficult issue to deal with since there are so many emotions involved. These feelings are often amplified when the situation affects other family members and children. The most important thing to do when facing domestic violence and abuse is to seek the right advice and support from the appropriate organization, whether this be the police, Women's Aid, Refuge or the Samaritans. These organizations have vast experience of dealing with domestic abuse and will be able to offer you the right advice for your particular situation. There will certainly be choices available to you and these could include:

- Individual counselling. This can either be face-to-face with a counsellor or you can speak to a counsellor over the telephone (contactable through the relevant organization) in complete confidence. Even if you just want to talk things over with someone – this is a good place to start.
- Joint counselling with the intention of repairing the relationship and thereby re-establishing trust.
- A temporary, or otherwise, separation.
- Reporting the abuse to the police, possibly obtaining a legal order which will force the perpetrator to remain a safe distance away from you.
- Contacting the appropriate organization – seeking a place of safety away from the domestic home.

If there are children involved, their safety is your priority. Remember to use your communication skills detailed in the previous chapters – these may help you to manage potentially dangerous situations or at least to reach a place of safety. Above all, realise that you are not alone – there are thousands and thousands of people who suffer/have suffered from domestic violence and abuse. There are also lots of people who want to and can help and contacting them is only a phone call away. You are also not to blame and although you may feel completely isolated and alone, the situation can be changed.

Telephone safety: landlines and mobile phones

The telephone can save your life in an emergency and can also be a cause of irritation. The following tips will be helpful to you:

1 If you don't have the following numbers near to your telephone **put them there NOW!** The next time you need an emergency number, you'll be thankful you spent the three minutes it takes to do it. You might also want to keep these numbers in your purse or wallet.

- the local police station
- the ambulance service
- the fire brigade
- your doctor.

2 When reporting an emergency, give the following information clearly:

- This is an emergency!
- Give your name.
- The nature of the emergency.
- The telephone number and address from which you are calling.
- The type of assistance that is necessary.
- For example: Hello operator, this is an emergency! My name is Cathy Spence and I am reporting a break-in at 24 Upside Down Street, Arbroath. The telephone number here is Arbroath 971234. Please send the police. Quickly!

Be sure you always have a suitable coin for making a telephone call every time you go out so you can call from a pay phone in an emergency. This may sound slightly old fashioned, particularly when telephone technology advances as we speak. Just as sure as little green apples exist, you may find yourself in this very situation: needing to use a coin-operated phone and having no coin in your pocket. Trust me: I have been in this very situation. The easiest way to do this is to keep a coin in a special place or in every pocket if you can and never use it for anything but an emergency. Alternatively, if you don't already own one, invest in a mobile telephone. Obtaining a mobile telephone is relatively easy and many companies offer inexpensive ways of running one. The important thing is to make sure it's kept charged and that there is credit on your phone, facilitating the making of a call.

Remember that when dialling the emergency services – **999** (UK) and **911** (USA) – you do not need any coins. This is the number for the emergency operator who will redirect your call to the emergency service necessary to respond to your call. The number **112** (UK) should be used for non-urgent calls to the police. You will be directed to an operator who will either give advice or take a brief report. You can also call your local police station direct but it's easier to remember **112**, which covers the whole of the United Kingdom.

If someone telephones your home, when you are alone and asks for your parents or spouse, say they're busy, perhaps in the toilet or shower, and cannot come to the phone. Take the caller's name and number and say the call will be returned. Never let unknown callers know you're alone.

When first answering the telephone simply say *Hello* and wait to hear who responds. If you don't recognize the voice ask *What number are you calling?* If the caller repeats an incorrect number, tell them it's the wrong number and then hang up. If you receive a wrong number, **never** give the caller yours, even if it appears to be a legitimate mistake.

A separate telephone with its own line and an unlisted or ex-directory number in another part of the house is an expensive option but it does offer special security. It might be the only way of calling for help during a burglary since most burglars take the first phone they see off the hook to prevent calls from extensions. Many households today have computers with broadband access to the Internet and, consequently, another line will always be available for phoning out.

How to deal with obscene telephone callers

Obscene callers, in case you've never heard from one, are people who fulfil their sexual fantasies by enticing unsuspecting people into sexual conversations over the phone. They often try to fool you by pretending to carry out a survey or saying that they know you. They usually start by asking harmless questions or sometimes they appear to be in trouble and appeal to your sympathy – **anything to get you involved in dialogue** – the punchline of which can often be their heavy breathing, lewd or rude dialogue. This can be quite upsetting and bothersome, and is potentially dangerous. In some cases, callers may compel you to do more than just talk. They'll try all their tricks to learn where you live or to get another clue that may lead them to you.

So, one very important rule is: **do not respond.** If you are at all suspicious about the caller's intentions or identity, hang up at once. This will usually take care of it, because obscene callers need a response to get their kicks or gratify their egos. Generally speaking, calls fall into two main classes: **silent calls,** during which the caller remains silent, so concealing their identity, and **verbal calls.** Statistics show that approximately 75% are of a silent nature and, in these cases, place the hand set beside the phone, go make yourself a cup of tea and then replace the handset some five or six minutes later. After all, it's the caller who is paying for the call. When answering the phone, say only *Hello* and wait for a response. Remember, **do not give your name or number.**

If the calls persist, the British Telecom Malicious Calls Bureau on **0800 661 441** can help. This bureau has an extremely high percentage (98%) of success. You may also, in serious cases, wish to contact the police to register an official complaint. In serious cases, the police will need to know the following:

- whether you know or recognize the voice
- whether it is male or female; perhaps giving some indication of age, accent
- what was said
- what times the calls were made at and how regular they are
- what measures you have taken to date.

Get an unlisted or ex-directory telephone number. If you must be listed in the phone book, only list your first initial – that way, it will not be obvious what gender you are. For example, if your name is Kathy Wilson, list your name in the book as K. Wilson. Your friends should know your number anyway, but if they forget, they can reach you through directory enquiries. There are additional precautions you can take to prevent unwanted and obscene calls, for example, invest in an answering machine and use it to screen your calls or consider the purchase of a caller display device, which allows you to see the caller's number before answering. These can be purchased from any good electrical store. Contact your telephone service supplier from whom you may be able to rent or buy one.

If you ever place an advertisement in the newspaper or on a notice/bulletin board and include your telephone number in it, do not give your first name or give any indication that you live alone.

Being a good neighbour

Join a neighbourhood watch scheme. Not only are these schemes worthwhile, they can have a dramatic effect on reducing your home insurance premium. Generally, these schemes involve neighbours looking out for each other. If you see any suspicious-looking persons, cars or activities in your area, call the police at once. Don't assume that someone else has called. Be as concerned for your neighbour's safety as your own – you may need to depend on it one day. If you see or hear anything unusual in or near a neighbour's house, call the police. Odd noises, a stranger taking a shortcut across your back garden or an unknown car parked with its motor running, may all appear to be minor things, but please consider that it is better to risk a false alarm than the safety of your neighbour. After all, you would want them to do the same for you. Don't give any information about a neighbour to someone you don't know and never tell strangers that your neighbour lives alone.

Computers

Most people in this technological world have a home or personal computer. As part of your home security plan keep a record of your computer serial number and think about the purchase of security cables that secure the computer to the desk thereby making it very difficult for a thief to remove the computer.

Online security is just as important as real security. Don't ever reveal your real name and address to anyone over the Internet. Use a screen name or pseudonym rather than your own. Never arrange to meet someone you met over the Internet in private. If you must meet up with someone you meet over the Internet, arrange to meet in a public place where there are lots of people and tell someone else you are making this arrangement. If you are a child and someone you do not know contacts you, do not reply. Report it immediately to your parent or guardian or other responsible person.

Hackers can view what you see on your screen and may also be able to access the information on your computer's hard drive. Ensure you install a good antivirus and anti-spyware software programme on your computer and run scans regularly. If you have a modem, check that it has a firewall configured to give additional protection when accessing the Internet and, more importantly, switch it on. If you must use credit cards for payment over the Internet try to ensure this is done via a secure server or use one of the other third party intermediary options, such as World Pay, PayPal, etc.

Identity theft

Identity theft is big business and it takes very little to impersonate you. Invest in a shredding machine to dispose of unwanted bank statements, credit card and store card accounts. Rifling through your garbage can tell a great deal about you and an identity thief will go to great lengths to find out as much as they can. Some people make a healthy living out of impersonating and defrauding others.

Personal identification numbers (PINs) are normally four-digit numbers applicable for using all credit cards. The compulsory introduction of these PINs on 14 February 2006 has dramatically reduced the incidence of fraud, with banks suggesting savings of up to 50 per cent against the normal loss. It is essential that these PINs are kept secret. Never reveal your PIN. Credit cards have a three or four-figure credit card verification (CCV) number on the back that you can quote to validate your use. Your PIN should be used at appropriate terminals. Make sure no one is looking over your shoulder to see your PIN. Avoid using your own date of birth. Consider using that of a parent or grandparent or another number you will readily remember. Your bank will tell you to keep the number secret and if you divulge it to anyone else the bank can refuse to reimburse you if transactions are made on your card without your knowledge. It's a case of buyer beware or, more correctly, cardholder beware. Never write the numbers down or keep them near to the card or in your wallet. Many people have written the number on the back of the card but this is just inviting trouble unnecessarily. Try to commit your numbers to memory. If you only have a few credit or store cards, a useful tip is to use the same number for them all.

Credential checking

Always select babysitters with the greatest of care. Only hire someone whom you can trust or who can provide you with personal references. Never hire anyone from an advertisement in a paper or magazine without first checking them out. If you can't find someone reliable with a good reference, contact a reputable agency. Before you leave anyone alone with your children, please be sure to check his/her credentials and identification thoroughly and explain any safety measures you may have to them, including where you can be reached in an emergency.

Letting anyone into your house without first checking their credentials is never good practice. One of the most dangerous automatic responses of which many of us are guilty is answering the door without first verifying the identity of the caller. Thieves and rapists can pose as repairmen, deliverymen or salesmen for an easy opportunity to enter your home. Always verify the identity of salesmen, workmen and even policemen before admitting them into your home. These people expect to be asked for their identity and they must always carry proper identity cards, so they won't be offended. Whenever the door bell rings, try to follow these precautions:

- Ask who's calling.
- Look through the safety viewer. Use the intercom.
- If you do not recognize the caller and what he claims to represent (e.g. the gas board), make sure the safety chain is secure.
- Open the door a few inches, use a door chain and place your foot against the door in case the person tries to burst in.
- Ask for identification.
- If anything seems suspicious, close the door and call the police immediately.

Never leave your door unlocked or open when workmen are around or if you're expecting a delivery, because you are only making it easy for a thief or assailant to slip in unnoticed. It is also very traumatic coming home to find your house has been broken into.

Action at a housebreaking

What to do if your home is broken into or you find a burglar in your house...

If you come home and find windows or doors broken or open **DO NOT GO INSIDE**. Without making too much noise, leave again at once and call the police from a nearby telephone, perhaps from a neighbour's house or your mobile and then wait for them to arrive.

If you suspect a criminal, jealous boyfriend/girlfriend etc. might enter your flat or your house during your absence, place a small piece of paper at the bottom of the door between the door and the door jamb. If the paper has gone when you return, it's likely someone has been in. **DO NOT GO INSIDE**; again call the police. This practical alert really works.

If you find yourself face to face with a burglar in your home, co-operate with them. Burglars caught are like trapped rats: they will do anything to escape. Do not attempt to hide valuables. Do not attempt tackling the burlar yourself.

But do attempt to...

Get a good look at the burglar in order to be able to give a good clear description to police. Some of the identification points listed in Table 4.1 will be useful to help you describe a person. Observe if anything has been touched or moved so that it can be forensically examined for fingerprints, glove prints, blood spills etc., which can later be used as evidence. Get a description of any car used, write down the registration number, colour and make a note of what direction the car leaves in. Note also if there are any other occupants in the car. Give all this information to the police. As soon as the burglar has left, lock all the doors and call the police. Make sure that neither you nor anyone else touch anything in the house or goes into any room where the burglar has been. Keep everything **exactly as it was** when the burglar left.

Sex	Male/female
Race	White/Caucasian, black African, Asian, Pakistani/Indian, Chinese, etc.
Hair	Long/short/wavy/straight/curly/bald/Afro/bushy/ unkempt/wig/crewcut/skinhead/dyed/thin
Amputee	Leg/arm/foot/hand/fingers/ears
Deformity	Leg/arm/hand/foot/fingers/bowlegged/knock knees/limp
Eyes	Missing/crossed/glasses/squint/bulging/blinking/ sunglasses

Identifying marks	Scars/tattoos/pockmarks/birthmarks/freckles/moles/pimples/piercings
Nose	Broad/big/small/thin/crooked/upturned/hooked/flat/broken
Complexion	Dark/sallow/ruddy/light/fair/medium
Teeth	White/yellow/stained/gold/missing/false/protruding or bucked/irregular
Facial hair	Beard (full or part)/moustache/goatee/unshaven/clean shaven
Face	Broad/thin/high cheek bones/round/chubby/long
Body	Large/medium/small/petite/slender/slim/chubby/obese
Ears	Big/small/protruding/pierced/cauliflower/close to the head
Speech	Foreign/stammer/stutter/impediment/fast/slow/slurred
Scars or burn marks	Where on body

table 4.1 identifying a suspect

Whenever you are away from your home, even if you're just going out for the evening, leave a light on and maybe a radio too. If an opportunist thief thinks somebody's at home, they will try elsewhere. If you're going on holiday or will be away from home for an extended period, you might consider asking a good friend or relative to move in until you return. Acquaint your 'house sitter' with preventive safety measures, such as those previously described, including where to turn off gas, electricity and water in the event of an emergency.

If you can arrange the following it will make your house seem occupied:

- Tell the Post Office to hold all your mail until further notice.
- Cut off all regular deliveries such as newspapers, milk, laundry, etc.

Don't give a reason for the above – this would be counterproductive. There have been cases where the milk delivery boy divulged this information to his friends who then made a call to the house and helped themselves to the contents. You never know who might make use of this information. You can always resume deliveries on your return. Let your local police officers know you'll be away and tell them where you can be reached in an emergency. They will monitor your house periodically and will be alert to any suspicious activity around your house.

Don't signal you're away by allowing your property to become run down in your absence. Arrange for someone you trust to check the property and make sure it stays in good condition. Lawns and hedges should be kept trimmed and in good shape and outside lights should be kept in working order. You can also buy an electrically powered timer at DIY stores to turn lights on and off at different intervals. Make sure such timers are set for varying intervals – if the lights come on at 7pm every night, somebody casing the house will know you are away. Tell a neighbour or relative whom you trust that you're going away and ask them to contact the police if they see anything unusual near your home. Perhaps give them a key and ask them to check occasionally. You might also ask them to change the level of blinds or curtains. A reasonably clever crook will figure out the house is unoccupied if the blinds and curtains are always in the same place. Don't announce your house is empty by taping notes to the door. This is a big no no. Prior to departure, lock all doors, check all windows are securely locked and remember to lock the garage.

If you own a company or have company responsibilities, make sure your colleagues know how to respond to questions about your whereabouts. The advice to give out is you are in a meeting but will call back when you are free. A business contact will normally identify themselves or be known to your colleagues. Burglars often call places of business to check whether someone is on holiday.

Keeping valuables, handbags and rucksacks

It is not recommended to keep large sums of money at home, particularly in cookie jars, jewellery boxes or under the mattress. If you must keep money around for one night, the safest place for it is in the freezer, packed neatly away in an airtight ice cream container. Unless the burglar develops a case of the 'super-munchies', your money is safe. Not only is the freezer one of the last places a burglar would look in, in the case of a fire the freezer is one of the best insulated areas in your home. Most modern chest freezers are lockable.

Expensive jewellery or other valuables should be kept in a bank safety deposit box and not at home unless in a safe installed at your house. It's a good idea to photograph your jewellery and other valuables to aid identification if they go missing or are stolen. If you have any clothing made of fur, remember that it is very difficult to identify furs when labels and linings have been removed, which is often the case with stolen furs. To counteract this, mark the insides of the skins in several places with your initials, social security number, postcode or a personal identification mark made up by you for the purpose of identifying your property. This rule is also true for other items such as bicycles, electronic goods, sports equipment, etc. Buy a special indelible marker pen from a hardware store and mark everything that can be stolen. For a couple of pounds, you can purchase an electric marker from a good DIY store and permanently etch your identification mark on all your appliances and valuables. If the goods are stolen, this identification aids their recovery. Without it, stolen items are untraceable and cannot be returned to you even if they are recovered. If the police cannot prove the articles are stolen they may have to return them to the suspect. Prosecution of criminals is difficult without real evidence, such as property that is clearly and identifiably yours. Make a complete record of all your equipment and valuables today. Note down serial numbers and remember to put everything down, from blenders to bicycles. Don't just list what can be taken away: many homes have been completely emptied, including cooker, doormat, the whole lot – and all when the owners were away for the weekend. Keep your list in a safe place, where you can find it, in the unfortunate event that you need it.

Important papers such as wills, birth certificates, stock certificates, passports, etc. should be stored in a bank safe deposit box or safe. Never store documents in the loft because during a fire it's likely they will be completely destroyed.

Always hold on tightly to your handbag and buy one with several zipped compartments in which you can place your money, purse, wallet, etc. As a general rule don't carry a lot of cash or expensive jewellery around with you unless this is absolutely necessary. If you must carry money and you're afraid of being robbed wear a money belt. During a self defence course I once taught, a female participant suggested pinning a money pouch to the inside of her underwear. This may be a good idea for a night out but retrieving it when at the local supermarket checkout having done your shopping might prove a little trying!

When choosing a handbag, look for one with a secure catch, preferably the type that requires more than one action to open it. Try always to carry your handbag with the opening next to your body. This will make it difficult for the pickpocket to get into if you are jostled. Try to keep your handbag or briefcase with you at all times. Don't put it down on the counter or inside your shopping trolley. Don't leave it on a chair while you try on a jacket or look through garments in a clothing store: sure as eggs is eggs, it will go missing. In restaurants, cinemas and theatres or on the bus, keep it on your lap, then you'll know exactly where it is.

Security in public places

Using lifts

When using the lift in high-rise properties you need to bear in mind that it can be stopped between floors and, if this happens, you will be caught in a trap. You should always be alert when using them. If you're waiting for a lift and someone in it looks at all suspicious, don't go in, just wait until the next one comes. If a suspicious-looking person gets in after you enter, leave at the next possible opportunity and wait until the lift comes around again. Be sure that the lift is going in the desired direction before entering. If there is anyone inside ask if it's going up or down. Never go in the opposite direction. It may take you to where a would-be assailant may be waiting, just for you. If you are alone in the lift with a stranger, stand next to the control buttons, so you can push the alarm button quickly if you have to – or, of course, the button for the next floor, so you can get out.

In the street

When walking down the street on your own, you must be aware of potential dangers. Avoid groups of noisy teenagers congregating on a corner or outside a shop. Simply cross the road and continue your journey. Don't let them see you are in any way afraid by turning around to look back. Using the reflection in shop windows to see who is behind you while walking alone in the street is a good ploy. Walk in safe areas where it's well lit and there are lots and lots of people – **seek people**. No attempt should be made to go onto empty train platforms or bus stations unless absolutely necessary. Standing next to people quietly waiting nearby can reduce risk significantly.

Buy a dog! This might not be the most practical of things to do, particularly if you live in a high-rise block or in an inner-city area, however, most opportunists will tend to give you a wide berth in fear of being bitten by the dog. Make sure the dog is trained to obey you. The last thing you want is the dog attacking you.

Beware of wearing tight and revealing clothes if you are out alone, particularly at night. It is a widely held misconception that wearing brief or revealing clothes means the wearer is promiscuous. Any person walking home late at night might attract the wrong or unwelcome attention, but if a woman is scantily dressed or provocatively attired, this risk is increased greatly. If you cannot avoid being out of doors late at night, reduce the risk by wearing a baggy coat to cover up party clothes.

If you must walk in dimly lit or unsafe areas, carry a noisemaker or a personal siren/alarm in your hand. Get an alarm and **keep it on your person**. Each alarm comes complete with a small cord you pull out to activate it. Do not attach the cord to your bag or belt because once the alarm is pulled from the cord, in a struggle your bag will be the first thing you will drop. This draws any attention to the alarm and not to you – and you may have moved away from the sounding alarm. **Keep it on your person!** Alarms can be purchased from catalogue stores and good DIY and hardware stores. It is not advisable to carry sharpened combs, sprays, coshes and the like, not only because it's against the law but because it is likely an assailant can turn them against you.

Clubbing

Alcohol and drugs

When you are out at a nightclub or in a bar be aware of those around you, particularly if they are unfamiliar to you. Beware of someone putting any substance in your drink. This is easy to do with an open glass and can be a wilful, wanton or malicious act. If using a glass is unavoidable, don't drink from it once you have put it down and left it unattended. You cannot be sure that the glass still contains what you left in it. Consider using bottles with a very narrow opening.

Remember, safety is in numbers and so it is always best advice to go along with friends. Electing one of you to guard the drinks is a good idea but even this is not foolproof. A small distraction is an opportunity for the determined perpetrator. It is very easy to make such a distraction and then spike a drink with either drugs or another form of alcohol which might render you incapable.

Alcohol slows down your reactions and can cause confusion. Many consider it to be the silent attacker. It takes very little to change the properties of a drink and, as many readers will be able to testify through their own experiences, mixing alcoholic drinks is a recipe for regret. Resist attempts from others to drink more than you ought to. You cannot be sure about their intentions – are they simply being friendly or are they actually being mischievous? Consume alcohol only within your known limitations. You can never defend yourself properly if you find it hard to stand or co-ordinate your limbs. Be alert to changes in others' behaviour especially if they seem controlling. If you suspect trouble or see a commotion, leave immediately and return home.

Put your coat and any valuables in the cloakroom. These places are secure and are manned by staff. This will prevent pilfering and theft of your property which could happen if you leave them unattended.

Bouncers – door stewards

These individuals are often seen in a bad light because when trouble kicks off they are the ones who have to deal with it, still sober, while others around them are in a heightened state of excitement. Their job can be a difficult one and their responsibilities include crowd control, security and stewarding in the event of an evacuation. They are not localized policemen for the premises; they exist to be of assistance to you. They have no more legal powers than any other common man but act on the authority of the licensee who must to abide by current local legislation. Most try to do their job in a conscientious manner. Modern local licensing legislation has made a big difference to the regulation of the door steward industry. Door stewards are now required to undergo training and have insurance before applying to the local authority for a licence. This means any actions consequential to carrying out their duties may have a detrimental effect on the licence for the premises. Local licensing courts can withdraw the licence from premises if the stewards are found to be heavy handed or negligent in their duty. This is in addition to any crime committed and dealt with by the legal courts.

One method employed by stewards in dealing with problems is to talk people down and calm the situation rather than encourage them to continue to do something stupid. This is called **de-escalation**. Often when under the influence of alcohol inhibitions are lowered and it can be difficult to behave in a proper manner and make rational decisions. Revellers don't often respond appropriately because they are in a heightened state of excitement or anxiety or under the influence of alcohol and consequently not thinking rationally.

Another method employed is to intervene to quell a disturbance and isolate perpetrators by ejecting them from the premises. In more serious situations, the police are called. If anyone is detained by the stewards it is under a **citizen's arrest**. Only the police have the authority to make a legal arrest.

Dating

Dating takes many forms but, in essence, it is part of the mating ritual preamble. This can be a very enjoyable experience or a series of disasters. It is difficult to predict what anyone will do but it's not rocket science to know that sexual fulfilment can be the real intention. And this is where safety considerations must come into play. A sweeping statement often voiced is that males are only looking for sex while females prefer to be romanced. In reality dating is a more complex series of behaviours with either sex being dominant.

Dating can commence in many ways: a smile, a sensual glance, a chance meeting. Normally it involves two people who want to get to know each other and who consent to explore their mutual company. Many dates never amount to anything while others extend to the blissful relationships envied by writers of romantic fiction and poets.

Internet dating can be fraught with safety problems. Some sites charge a fee as a form of membership to access databases of those seeking partners – and this may be a sufficient deterrent for a casual fraudster. However, online dating in general is a proverbial minefield because you never know who you are talking to unless you actually know them personally or are connected to a live video link. Anyone can assume a false identity and with the correct language make you believe that they are someone else. Impersonation is commonplace on the Internet and without any form of policing it leaves you very vulnerable. Many people see participation in chatrooms to be harmless because they can express themselves in whatever way they wish while hiding behind a pseudo character. This can take the form of escapism or a harmless fantasy or role play but lives have been destroyed in the process. It's good advice to ensure that if you must arrange a date over the Internet that it is through a reputable agency.

However you meet your date, it pays to follow some basic safety rules. Arrange to meet in a public place where there are plenty of people. Remember, seek people; safety in numbers. It might be that the person is not as you envisaged and you need an escape plan. Make sure you tell someone where you intend going, who you are meeting and when you intend returning. Also give instructions that if you do not make contact by a certain time to alert the police.

Rape and sexual assault

Rape is a crime defined in common law as *the carnal knowledge of a woman forcibly and against her will whether consent is given or not.* There are additional statutory offences ranging from sex with minors to what is effectively sodomy (male rape). Rape is a violent act and the sexual act is not thought to be the overriding intention.

Rape as a crime has seen a great deal of public interest in recent years, both in the media and by criminologists. The legal debate has always centred on whether a woman has given her consent and this has to be measured against other evidence such as a struggle and whether there was any penetration.

One significant change recently is the way in which the law views how a woman gives consent or not. The Law Lords have recently upheld in a stated case (H.M.A – v – James Wright 2005) that women who engage in activity which is likely to result in sexual intercourse and who, due to high consumption of alcohol, cannot give consent have effectively given their consent.

This has profound implications for women who enjoy consuming large amounts of alcohol in that the law may not now provide them with the protection they once had if someone tries to engage them in sexual activity under the influence.

Psychologists and criminologists have believed for many years that rape and sexual assault is always more about power and control used to degrade and dominate the victim rather than fulfilling a sexual desire; this would explain why often the rapist is known to the victim. The crimes of rape and sexual assault are not always committed with brutal force, the instances of date rape drugs being used are on the increase.

Date rape drugs can be easily slipped into a drink or food and the effects can be very powerful and dangerous. Victims who have been subject to this have reported being fully conscious, sensing everything, but not having any ability to physically move. These drugs act upon the neuromuscular system and incapacitate the recipient.

- **GHB** – Short for gamma-hydroxybutyrate, GHB is most often administered as a clear liquid with a salty taste, but can also be found in capsule and powder forms.
- **Ketamine** – Administered in liquid, tablet and powder form, Ketamine is a fast-acting general anaesthetic often used by veterinarians.
- **Rohypnol** – Often dropped into beverages in tablet form, Rohypnol is a potent and fast-acting sedative that dissolves rapidly, leaving no detectable taste, colour or odour.
- Be aware that the most common date rape drug is **alcohol**. So beware what you drink, and how much, and be a good friend – look out for each other. If you start feeling the effects of alcohol, don't accept another drink.

When out, watch your drink at all times.

With regard to the action one should take when faced with a potential rape or sexual assault, it is very easy in the cold hard light of day to extol views on the action one might take when faced with these situations but a completely different matter when actually faced with these crimes in real life – you never know how you are going to react until the situation happens. However, interestingly, there are two main views 'extolled' by those considering their possible action to such crimes – firstly, those who think they would act 'passively', stating that they do not consent to the sexual act but not offering any physical resistance to the perpetrator either out of shock or fear of making the situation even worse. Secondly, those who think they would react physically, fighting until the bitter end irrespective of the consequences or injuries. Those who argue that the second approach is more likely to deliver the desired outcome (reaching safety) claim that a percentage of those who resist strongly are raped whereas those who don't resist are all raped. Regardless of the view you hold prior to an attack, it is of utmost importance that you trust your instincts – if you feel uncomfortable in a situation, try and reach a place of safety as soon as possible, use your assertiveness skills, scream for help, run away, use the physical protocols described in this book.

What to do if you have been raped

It is strongly advised that you contact the police immediately after an attack – although this is obviously your choice. You should give a good description or, if known, reveal the identity of the person responsible. Time will be of the essence because biological evidence such as DNA profiling can be destroyed or deteriorate as time elapses. Many women over the years have bathed after such a horrific attack and this is quite understandable, but it also destroys evidence likely to convict a rapist. Ultimately victims of rape may undergo a medical examination to ascertain injuries and will include collection of evidence, for example, body fluids, hair, skin etc., for DNA testing. Such tests can confirm the existence of date rape drugs in the bloodstream or urine.

There are numerous organizations such as Women's Aid and the Samaritans who are there to offer support and advice – you can either speak to someone face-to-face or phone the helpline in complete confidence. It can be very difficult to disclose something so repugnant and innumerable women have kept a rape or an assault a secret, often until something sparks off a memory leading to disclosure. But rape and sexual assault, whether by a stranger or a friend, is never the victim's fault. The police and other organizations are here to help you.

The sexual nuisance, groper or exhibitionist

Sexual nuisances can be either male or female. More often than not they sidle up to you in a bar, club or train and try to engage you in conversation and make you instantly feel uncomfortable or 'freaked out'. There may be many reasons why you feel uncomfortable, most likely they are invading your space and exuding an aura or intention that you do not feel happy with or feel threatened by, but it is worth considering that you may have social prejudices of your own that make you feel like this – perhaps you feel uncomfortable around older/younger men or women? Regardless of the reasons behind your anxiousness, you must act appropriately and quickly – be polite, if you do not want to enter into conversation make your excuses and leave the company. If the stranger persists to annoy you with advances, leave and arrange for someone to come and meet you – seek other people. If he/she follows you, call the police with your mobile phone or go directly to a police station. I firmly believe that if you don't want to tango, don't get up to dance so trust your instincts – if you feel uncomfortable do something about it, don't let the situation get worse.

Dealing with someone who displays 'wandering hand' trouble at a bar or in a confined space such as a lift or toilet area can be equally distressing. Touching is a very intimate activity and social and moral rules dictate that permission is obtained prior to the act. We must remember that 'gropers' have no respect for the people they assault, and this is an assault. One sure fire way to deal with it is to bring lots of attention to the groper. These people like to act furtively and anonymously. They dislike the public attention being brought to their acts and so raising that attention may well stop them as well as recruiting assistance from those near to you.

If you see an exhibitionist or, as they are sometimes commonly described, 'flashers', the wisest tactic is to ignore them and contact the police. Do not laugh or make demeaning remarks such as *'I'm very sorry I have little time to deal with your shortcomings'*. This kind of response could anger and easily provoke a situation you would rather not be involved in. Exhibitionists can be of either sex, most are relatively harmless and you should report them to the police.

Travelling

If you are travelling by bus or train, try to learn the timings so you don't have to stand on an empty platform or a deserted corner for too long. If someone does in fact bother you, either on the bus or the train, report the incident to the driver or conductor. Avoid getting off if possible: a determined person will follow you. Most local bus drivers have radios and can call for help quickly. Try to travel with a friend whenever you can.

If travelling by taxi, check the identification of the driver and be sure it is, in fact, a taxi and not somebody pirating. All taxi drivers are regulated by the local authorities and carry identification. Perhaps consider sharing a taxi with friends. Not only is this economical, it is also safer – remember, safety is in numbers. You might also ask the taxi driver to wait until you are safely inside when you reach your destination, particularly if you have to negotiate a dark path or the like to get inside. Many taxi drivers are only too happy to be of assistance. You can also call your parents (where appropriate) or friends to let them know you are en route home and will call them again when you arrive there safely. If there is a problem, they can alert the authorities.

While it is not a good idea for children to be travelling alone, sometimes it can't be avoided, for example going to and from school, etc. If you are a child travelling alone, please remember not to talk to strangers and keep your mobile phone handy. If a stranger approaches you while on public transport, keep your wits about you and try to work out whether they are just giving you advice or whether they wish you harm. You can always try to contact the driver or conductor. Someone being nice to you doesn't always mean they intend to be so all the time. Don't ever go away with a stranger even if they say your parents said you should. Make a call on your mobile to either a friend or your parent. When children are travelling alone it is a good idea to arrange for someone to put the child on the form of transport and also someone else to meet them at the destination. Usually children are well catered for if it involves a flight. The airlines take great measures to ensure their safety while in their charge.

On holidays

The best-laid travel plans can end up in a disaster if you lose your travel documents, namely your passport or identification card, visa or travel tickets. Replacing these documents is not easy and can cause a great deal of stress, not to mention result in disastrous travel often cut short by repatriation. Keep your travel documents safe on your person; don't place them in a bag or rucksack that can be stolen. If your documents are stolen or go missing, report this immediately to the appropriate authorities: the police in the first instance, the passport office and then your own national embassy where they will normally arrange to have an emergency passport provided for you.

Arrive a little earlier than the stated travel departure time to avoid losing your place. Many cheaper airlines have a policy to oversell their allocation of seats and many passengers are inconvenienced every year as a result.

Carry only a little currency with you. Use traveller's cheques rather than cash or, indeed, carry a credit card. If you need to carry money, put it in a concealed pocket that has a zip fastener making it difficult for a pickpocket to steal from you. Don't forget to arrange appropriate travel insurance when travelling. Make sure it covers your personal belongings, replacement travel documents, repatriation of your remains, sporting cover, delay or curtailment, etc. The clear message is **check the small print**. There is nothing worse than finding out your policy does not cover what you think it does. **Check before you go!** Finally, before you go make a note of your passport numbers, travellers' cheques numbers, credit card numbers, etc. and deposit these with a trusted person whom you could contact in an emergency. It will be important to have all those details to hand when making a report.

Hitchhiking

You'd be shocked at the number of young men and women who get into trouble when hitchhiking. By hitchhiking, I refer to an activity that is carried out on roads, involving people hitching a lift with a strange driver to their destination.

Hitchhiking is undoubtedly a dangerous activity – I do not recommend it. However, I know that many people do it so I have included advice for those who do decide to travel in this way. Making the decision to hitchhike may not be the best decision but at least this advice will lend its way to making you safer and at least limit your risk. Hitchhiking is both popular on the European continent and in the USA but in the United Kingdom it's less so. While it's considered a popular and inexpensive way to get around and see a country, there are hazards which you need to be aware of and try to avoid. Many of these hazards apply also to backpackers.

Safety

Although hitchhiking is more hazardous than bus or train travel, it's still considered statistically to be safer than many other forms of transport such as cycling. (This information is based on declared statistics comparing reported accidents involving both activities.) This doesn't mean anyone should give up cycling in favour of hitchhiking. The most dangerous thing about hitchhiking is the possibility of being involved in a car accident or being hit by a car if you stand too close to the side of the road and so it's important to choose a safe spot to hitchhike. It's a good idea to get to the outskirts of town or city, to a road leading to a motorway (expressway). Pick a spot with plenty of room for the driver to stop safely. If possible, try to stand where the traffic isn't moving too quickly because it's safer and most drivers want to size you up before deciding whether to pick you up. If you've got a ride on a motorway, get dropped off at a service area where you'll have facilities like a restaurant, shop and toilets. You can chat to and ask truck drivers about getting a ride. Don't hitchhike on the actual motorways, stick to the entrance ramps and service areas. Not only is hitching on motorways dangerous, in most places it's illegal – vehicles are not allowed to stop on the motorway unless directed by a police officer or traffic sign.

There is also, of course, a danger posed by accepting a ride from a driver you do not know. The driver could either be a dangerous character or simply a bad driver. Despite the perceived danger, there are plenty of ways in which to minimize your risk. If you're a single female hitchhiker you'll attract your fair share of attention from obnoxious drivers. It's a better idea to travel with someone else, preferably a male. This way you'll be seen as a couple, which means that you shouldn't have any sleazy men trying to come on to you and if they do at least there is someone to help you out.

A really good tip is to plan your route carefully. Remember to inform someone, the country rangers (if you are backpacking), a relative, a trusted friend, of your route and expected estimated times of arrival at checkpoints. It will be important to keep in touch with these people to update them on your progress. If you are in trouble the early alert from them to the emergency services may just save your life.

Consider carrying a mobile phone and only go where there is reception – your phone will indicate this – since being able to call for help obviously makes travelling safer. This is particularly so when in the countryside where there may not be good reception for your phone. Your service provider can advise you on the coverage in any area you are travelling in. For this method to work keep your phone charged and in your pocket; you also need to know the emergency number (**112** is the international emergency number from GSM mobile phones, **911** in the United States and throughout the British Isles the emergency number **999** should be used). Consider taking a spare battery for your phone if you are spending a long time out of communication. For those going further afield where telephone coverage is not possible consider carrying a two-way radio or satellite phone to keep in touch. Units can be large, however, depending on the make and model.

Don't let the driver put your backpack or luggage in the boot or stowage area of the vehicle. Try to keep all your belongings with you, even when you stop for food and fuel. Don't feel compelled to accept a ride just because someone has stopped for you. If it doesn't feel right, don't get in. Another ride will come along. You'll find a lot of opportunities to hitch a ride come from regular stoppers.

Drivers will have many different reasons for picking you up: drivers who've perhaps hitchhiked themselves and are repaying the favour, frequent solo drivers like couriers and truck drivers who want some company. To improve your chances of finding someone responsible to give you a ride, consider the following:

1 Look neat and respectable. It's important you look non-threatening to any driver.

2 Face the oncoming traffic and smile. It's important that people can see your face, so try to avoid wearing sunglasses.

3 Try to look smart and clean, but don't overdo it. You don't want to give the wrong impression or attract the wrong attentions.

4 When a vehicle stops, ask the driver where he is going to. At this point it's easy to decline the ride if you don't like the look of the driver or if they aren't heading towards your final destination.

5 Never smoke in someone else's vehicle.

6 Travel light. The lighter your load, the easier it is to get around.

7 If you too are a driver, carry your driver's licence. Some drivers stop because they want someone to share the driving. The main issue here is to make sure that you are covered to drive by insurance before doing so. Every country has different driving regulations, so check before you go.

The important message is to be safe and a good way to do that is keep in regular contact with relatives who you can update on your whereabouts. I cannot condone hitchhiking, but if you go ahead I recommend that you take all necessary precautions as detailed in this section.

However, if any doubt persists – don't go.

Motorists' security

Car drivers need to be just as alert about maintaining their safety when driving as anywhere else. If you have any doubts, never give a lift to someone you don't know – you might be compromising your personal security to an assailant. Drivers are advised to ensure they comply with the law in respect of wearing seatbelts. Children must use car seats and booster seats where applicable.

Your car should always be in good working order. Check the tyres, battery, water, oil, fanbelt and water hoses periodically. Be sure that your petrol tank is always at least one-quarter full and carry a torch in your car. You'll appreciate the extra time spent on these precautions when you have to drive alone or if you have to go out at night. Always try to ensure that doors are locked and windows closed when driving alone. You can use the car's ventilation system to regulate the temperature, but if you want a window open, make it the one next to you so you can close it quickly, if you have to.

Contrary to what the Highway Code states, your car **should be in gear**, even when you've stopped at the traffic lights. If you feel you're in trouble or have to get away fast, bear down on the horn and drive away. Always try to drive on main roads. Don't use lightly travelled roads if there is an alternative route. If you see a car following you, don't drive home, drive to the nearest police station, filling station or garage, whichever is closest. Familiarize yourself with those filling stations or garages that are open 24 hours. If the car follows you there and doesn't leave within a reasonable time, ask the attendant to call the police. If a car that's following you tries to pull you over to the side of the road, don't pull over, or try to shake him off. Get a careful note of the registration number and description of the car and driver if possible and then drive straight to your nearest police station. Keep a notepad and pen handy in your car for such situations. If it's too far or you don't know where it is, drive to a nearby place of business where you can phone the police. Alternatively, stop your car and call the police via your mobile phone. Remember not to use your mobile phone while driving unless it's configured for hands-free use.

Join an automobile club or association that can help you if your vehicle breaks down. If you spend a lot of time driving in any day, consider investing in a mobile phone or a car phone. Both the AA and the RAC have mobile phone schemes linked to their switchboards and, in addition, have arrangements to assist lone women drivers or mothers with children who are stranded or need mechanical help. You do not need to be a member of either organization to make use of this emergency arrangement.

Stranded motorist

If you are stranded in your car, on a secondary road and you can see a filling station or telephone nearby, switch on the hazard flashing lights of your car and tie a white cloth or a handkerchief to the aerial. Lock your car and walk towards the filling station, preferably facing the traffic. On motorways and some dual carriageways you can, of course, use the emergency telephones dotted along the roadside at about one-mile intervals. These phones are direct links to the police. If you stop and are not sure which way the nearest phone is, look for little pegs stuck into the ground about a foot or so high on the side of the hard shoulder. They can be easily seen by their reflective capabilities. These pegs have little arrows on the top to indicate the direction of the nearest phone. If your car has broken down on the motorway get out and use the telephones available. Return to your car but stay on the verge behind the crash barriers. Other drivers can collide with your stationary car and if you are inside you are at greater risk of injury. Stay on the verge to the front of your vehicle. Remember that motorways and dual carriageways are patrolled at all hours.

If you happen to be stranded in the countryside or an isolated area during heavy rain or a storm, it is safer to stay **inside** your car. Open the window just a little for ventilation and run the engine at intervals for warmth. If someone stops to assist you, make sure your car is locked, with you inside. Roll the window down an inch or so and ask them to phone for assistance. Don't leave your car and don't accept a ride from the motorist. Many criminals take advantage of unsuspecting people unfamiliar with the area and lead them to desolate places where they can rob or attack them. Never stop to help a stranded motorist. Call the police from the nearest phone. You cannot know if someone is genuinely in trouble or if it is a ploy to lure you into a trap.

Don't leave your driving licence, the car's MOT certificate, registration or the insurance documents in the glove compartment. This is only helping car thieves identify themselves as you if stopped by the police. Keep them at home in a safe place. If police need to see your documents they will issue you with a ticket (HO/RT1) to produce the documents within a specified period of time (normally seven days) at your nearest police station. So while it's technically against the law not to produce them right away, the law provides that as long as you do produce them within a specified period, it is okay.

Don't leave your belongings, especially valuables, lying in plain full view. Lock them away in the boot or conceal them under the seats. Your handbag or wallet should never be on the seat next to you while driving. Put it either in the glove compartment or on the floor opposite you. All car accessories, for example your radio or compact disk player or removable parts, should be marked with your driving licence number or your postcode to aid identification in the event of their being stolen. If you find your car broken into, call the police at once. A good sign is to check that the rubber window seal just above the lock is still in place and has not been tampered with.

You should always carry a record of your licence number and car registration number on a separate piece of paper in your purse or wallet. If your car is then stolen, report the incident to the police immediately and give them these details.

Many modern cars have central locking and factory-fitted alarms but others don't. **NEVER** leave your car unlocked; a few moments may be all a car thief needs. When driving at night, always park your car in an attended car park or in a well-lit, busy area, unless you are able to park right outside your destination, otherwise lock it in your garage. Be alert when returning to your car. Have your car keys ready in your hand and check to see that no one is following you. Make sure there is no one hiding in the back seat. Get in quickly and lock the door. When you return home, leave the headlights on until you open the garage. Park the car, lock the garage and unlock the door to your house. Remember to leave lights on at the garage and at your front entrance before you leave and they'll be on when you return. Garages of apartment buildings or multistorey buildings are particularly vulnerable, so be especially alert when entering one. It's always a good idea to arrange for someone you know to meet you at the entrance if possible.

Finally, **DO NOT LET CRIME PAY**. Be alert and aware of your surroundings. If you see something unusual, don't shrug it off, no matter how minor it appears, report it to the police immediately. It may help prevent a crime. Look out for your neighbour's welfare, as you would want them to look out for yours.

Summary

Here are six little golden rules to remember:

1 Do not encourage members of the opposite sex if you have no intentions of playing a sexual game.
2 Do not find yourself alone with a suspicious character.
3 Do not walk down dark streets alone. If you must, keep away from doorways and openings. Have an escape route planned.
4 Seek people! The lone menace will not attack in a crowd.
5 Avoid any place that has a reputation for violence or unruly behaviour.
6 When faced with a dangerous situation, follow the cardinal rule – **DON'T PANIC**.

Don't forget to make a note of bank account, credit card, passport, important documents numbers and serial numbers of valuables in your home. **DO IT NOW** and keep this list safe. Most of what has been said here, if not everything, is basic common sense but just consider how many of us actually fail to use this sense of ours. Adopting these simple suggestions into your daily life can make a difference to your safety.

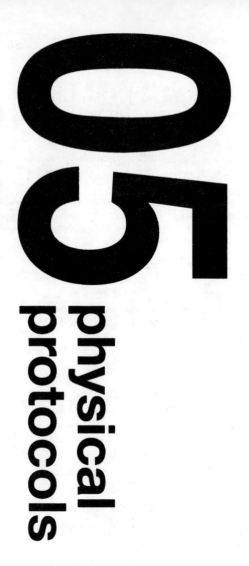

05 physical protocols

In this chapter you will learn:
- four golden rules of self defence
- where to strike an assailant for best effect
- how to deal with common attacks.

We are now going to examine and learn some physical self defence techniques that can be put into practice if you ever need to defend yourself.

Learn to practise and then practise to learn. I have always found this a helpful maxim. It is very important that you work through the physical techniques in this chapter step by step, practising each technique over and over until the physical action resembles something like a real-life situation. This type of practice builds your confidence, increases your abilities and facilitates your development. The techniques contained in this section are all left and right hand compliant. This means that they can be performed on either side with the same effect.

Before we start practice, there are some golden rules that need to be considered. These rules are based on common sense and they are fundamental to personal safety and self defence.

Four golden rules

Rule 1: train for action

Those who want to learn self defence must first be in the right frame of mind and realize that their training must start slowly and deliberately until they mirror closely the scenarios found in real life. You'll need to expose yourself to this kind of training so that you can fend off an attack at any time and anywhere. This does not mean looking for opportunities to practise for real, simply that your practice or training becomes as near to the real thing in preparation for an eventuality. By doing this, you learn to react to what happens rather than academically thinking things through. In a physically hostile situation, you don't have the time to think.

Self defence requires a very different approach to that of boxing or a martial art. The aims of self defence training would be to have a useful product in only hours of training rather than spending months and months on it. Neither the teaching methods of boxing nor most of the techniques of traditional martial arts are really suitable for self defence training. This is because these systems generally include too many techniques. Our programme is quite concise and gets to the point quickly. It deals with the most common attack scenarios in a very simple, easy-to-learn way. The techniques used in this chapter should only be used in an emergency if you see no other way out of the situation but to resort to physical techniques. Avoid a fight if you can and don't engage in a mindless argument. You will need to have these techniques 'at your fingertips' so you will have to practise. I suggest you find a trustworthy friend or colleague to practise the techniques that I am about to give you.

Rule 2: keep it simple

It is a widely held misconception that only those who are very skilled in traditional martial arts can teach self defence. This is not true; many who are trained in the traditional forms of any oriental fighting art have not had the proper preparation to teach or even understand what is needed in a modern self defence class. Many of these 'experts' teach techniques that have no application in self defence, and have equally no use in the context of a self defence course. Consequently, the techniques do not work and this places you at a greater risk of injury. The physical protocols in this chapter have been carefully devised to ensure your safety. They really work!

The acronym **KISS** stands for Keep It Simple, Stupid. It embodies the essence of simplicity and true refinement. By keeping your mind free from catalogues of techniques and the traditional rules that bind martial artists, you are left with a routine you will find simple. One final note: action seen on films is all choreographed to be spectacular. Self defence is designed to be **effective**. There are neither awards to win nor rules to restrict you. Learn the step-by-step protocols in this book and you will be safer.

Rule 3: use only reasonable force

You also need to know about the law of the land in respect of what constitutes an assault and what is permitted as self defence. Generally, you should learn to do only what is necessary and is effective with reasonable force, otherwise you may end up facing a judge and charges of assault or worse (see Chapter 06). While martial arts have a large enough repertoire of techniques to accommodate any situation, the secret really lies in selecting the right techniques for the individual and situation. You are of a particular size and body shape and have a way of moving. So will any would-be attacker. Included in this the physical protocols chapter are a series of defensive measures to deal with the most common situations. But there is no hard and fast rule here; it will essentially be down to what suits the individual and what works for them.

Do not make the mistake of assuming that a nine-stone female is able to emulate the actions of a 14-stone male instructor who is demonstrating the technique. It may work for him with commensurate ease but it's unlikely to be the same for the nine-stone female trying to do the same. The problem in this instance is that the selection of techniques does not really work well, if at all. The difference between other programmes and the one detailed in this book is that the physical protocols of this book have been designed specifically with everyone in mind. There are no lifts, fancy kicks or footwork to master. These techniques work effectively!

Rule 4: engage only when necessary

There are three subgroups within this heading representing the possible action you can take. The first is **RUN**. It is important in all forms of self defence that exponents learn from a very early stage that engaging an opponent in combat must only be as a last resort. Running away or screaming to avoid engaging in a situation in the first place is a highly preferred option. Many develop a higher sense of awareness and often report of *sensing an incident* before it happens and then make themselves scarce. However, don't confuse this action with procrastination. Waiting to see if something pans out is simply stupid. Learn to trust your instincts. Effective self defence exponents act quickly and decisively and then extricate themselves from the situation as fast as possible. Funnily enough, it's only in the movies that the successful self defence exponent hangs around for the praise and accolades. In real life this never happens. When practising self defence techniques, the final result should be effective and spontaneous and not overly rehearsed. You ought to be able to move without thinking and deliver your techniques almost like a reflex. Reaction time will be crucial, as will technique selection and body positioning.

The second subgroup is **TALK**. Talking your way out is not the coward's way and does not involve you pleading for mercy, but cleverly using language to help the attacker see reason. This is where your use of good communication skills comes in. Confrontation is an aggressive interaction between two or more people. You react to a person, the person reacts to you. You can't control what someone else does but you can control what you do and by doing something positive, you will be able to influence the behaviour of others. This can have the effect of turning a difficult behaviour into a civilized constructive behaviour that facilitates both parties and others to think better of themselves. As stated in Chapter 03, this may go as far as telling them just what they want to hear or telling a blatant lie. There are many of us who feel guilty about telling a lie. We are brought up to understand that one lie begets another and leads to the slippery slope. Try using this **coping mechanism**. The objective is not to feel good about telling lies per se, but there is certainly no need to feel guilty when you have to tell a lie to protect yourself in the instance of danger, particularly when the content of the lie is not important.

The last grouping under this heading is **FIGHT HARD.** It is important you realize the value of fighting as hard as you can when you need to. Use your environment to help you. Look for obstacles that you can use to impede your attacker's way. Useful obstacles include bollards, walls, lamp posts, large rubbish bins, boxes, fences, etc. Put them between you and your attacker and run in the opposite direction. Whenever you find yourself in the situation of having to physically interact with another person, do it without fear or favour. The aggressor will certainly not take into consideration your frailty, whether you can fight or not, whether you are strong enough, etc. They simply don't care. Judge whether you ought to make a physical response and do it. Don't second guess yourself. In a serious attack it's more appropriate to respond by taking away your aggressor's ability to see or breathe rather than to cause a distraction in an attempt to escape. Attack the eyes or the throat to ensure effectiveness. Don't forget to shout and scream to attract attention.

Another specific technical aspect of self defence is the development of positional sense. This is an ability to know where to position yourself to maximize your best options. Making use of good positional sense will give you the ability to nullify some attacks while protecting yourself from others. This means effectively being in the correct place, at the right time and being able to execute the correct technique. This comes with experience and is an ability often developed at higher levels of practice, with the foundation work being carried out in the first sessions. Knowing when and how to escape will be the key. You must also know what is required should you meet an unexpected resistance. Using the resistance of an opponent against them is a skill in itself, one that I encourage you to find and exploit. (See the coaching tips at the end of each technique.) Your progress in these areas should be made incrementally according to your abilities. Outstrip your abilities and it will lead to the undermining of your confidence – quite contrary to our basic objectives.

Good luck!

Preparing for practice

Having recognized that learning self defence is important it is equally important to recognize the need to practise these physical protocols until they become second nature to you. Try to remember that practise makes permanent, not perfect. First, you need to find a training partner who can share your journey through learning the physical protocols. This will be vital to your success. Having a partner to share the ups and downs with as well as the hard work (and sometimes a little pain) is a valuable resource. A key for you both will be to respect each other. A simple and effective signal which should be used by you both is a double tap with a hand to indicate that the technique has been successful and you submit. This is a good safety measure to establish before you begin practice. The next consideration is where you practise. It is not necessary to go to a gym, you can practise within the confines of your home. Just make sure you are not likely to fall onto anything which may cause you injury. To begin with, wear something loose and comfortable when practising. This will become less important as you progress because if attacked you should be able to respond irrespective of what you wear.

It will also be useful to you to undergo some additional physical training to improve your general strength, endurance and physical well-being. You will be able to cope with an attack much better if you are in good shape. If you are fitter, your body will also be able to endure the bumps and bruises, which will heal quicker. More importantly, by feeling fitter you will have a more positive approach to your capabilities.

In preparation for practise you will need to do a gentle warm-up – this will prevent injury.

Warm-up and cool-down

Warm-up routines, as an aspect of training or performance, are a mixture of callisthenic exercises and sport-specific exercises, which will appertain to what the individual wishes to carry out at the intended session. The warm-up comprises of general exercises and specific exercises. Look at the warm-up as a modular system of exercises, strung together in a particular format to give the intended effect. Singularly, this aspect of your preparation is probably the most important part prior to practice. For practice, the warm-up will be specific to the work that you intend to carry out. There are three main components of a warm-up.

Cardio-pulmonary

This part should feature early in the warm-up and is designed to increase the blood flow and develop the ability of the lungs to take in oxygen and expel carbon dioxide in the primary phase. Whole body actions such as shaking your arms, hands, feet and legs – all at the same time – running on the spot, etc. these all elicit an increase in blood flow and tidal breath volume.

Mobilization

This part involves the systematic mobilization of joints and loosening of muscles prior to demand being placed on them. Gently and repetitively move each limb to the end of its range to warm up the muscle tendons and the joints.

Stretching

In this part, stretching is gentle and progressive as opposed to the more aggressive stretch to improve overall extensibility, which should be carried out at the very end of the training session. Stretch muscles in groups to begin with and then isolate individual muscles according to your own requirements.

The warm-up should not be excessively long – approximately 12–15 minutes of balanced exercises should suffice – and the approach should be systematic, i.e. starting off at the head or the feet and working through the body to the opposite end:

- Shake the hands and feet.
- Move all your limbs through their whole range of motion (ROM).
- Gently stretch these muscles through their ROM.
- Carry out the exercises until you begin to feel breathless or profuse sweat.
- Now you're ready for work.

After the warm-up you will be able to feel a distinct physical difference, for example heightened body temperature, increased heart rate, etc. and now practice can begin. Physical training, by way of contrast, will involve conditioning your muscles to carry out a specific function such as development of strength, speed, stamina or extensibility.

A word on cool-downs

Not that many sportspeople consider cool-down as relevant, yet it is just as important, if not more so, than the warm-up routine. Consider this: if your muscles are cold, then stretching is more likely to cause injury. Muscle needs to be warm to give a better ROM through its length. So, as logic would have it, any aggressive stretching session is more beneficial at the **end** of the training session. In reality, you will find incorporating a good stretching session at the end of your session will not only be an investment for the next one, it will assist the recovery of the muscle from the rigours of the training session and the evacuation of unwanted metabolites.

The recipe for your practice should consist of 10–15 minutes warm-up, 30–40 minutes during which the intensity threshold of your practice is exceeded and about 20 minutes cooling down. To begin with walk through each of the protocols to learn the sequence and, once conversant with them, have your training partner use a little more force to make it feel more like a real situation. Through this type of progressive practice your confidence will gradually increase and you learn what your abilities are rather than focusing on what you cannot do. Try to make your practice incremental by progressing step by step. Trying to learn too much at one go is a recipe for disaster. Likewise, if your partner uses too much force during the learning phase, it may have a negative result. You can become demotivated and discouraged. This is counterproductive. Have respect for each other!

The lessons

The following can be considered as core techniques just as English and Mathematics are considered as central in education. This core can then be tailored according to your needs. There are too many permutations to include everything in this book but this basic programme includes the main forms of attack and how to deal with them effectively. Remember that the ethos is to escape and run, **not** to fight. You must practise these techniques so that your skills become permanent.

Escapes from hand grabs

Let's look at two examples.

Single-hand grab

In this example your assailant has grabbed one of your wrists with his two hands. Let's follow the sequence: if an assailant grabs one of your hands or wrists by using both of his hands (Figure 5.1), irrespective of whether your assailant is much bigger than yourself, your action must be fast and, more importantly, effective. The method here is to lean forward, over your assailant, and take your own grabbed hand with your free hand (Figure 5.2). Keep the elbow of your held arm close to your body (Figure 5.3) as you move your weight back, away from your assailant (Figure 5.4). At the same time pull your hand sharply back against the assailant's thumbs to free your hand.

Summary

- Lean forward

- Grab your trapped hand

- Step back

- Pull it free

- Run away

Coaching points

- Keep your elbow in close to your body.

- Step back and use your body weight to good effect.

- A sharp jerk is far better than a slow strong pull.

- Last tip: **don't** hold your breath.

figure 5.1 single-hand grab (1)

figure 5.2 single-hand grab (2)

figure 5.3 single-hand grab (3)

figure 5.4 single-hand grab (4)

Double-hand grab

In this example your assailant has grabbed both of your wrists, one in each of his hands. If each of your hands (Figure 5.5) are held by the same assailant the action is straightforward. Swiftly kick to your assailant's groin (Figure 5.6) which will have the effect of releasing the grip on your hands. Run away from the assailant, screaming.

Summary

- Kick the groin
- Run
- Scream

Coaching points

- Don't be afraid to kick the groin hard. It will be necessary to make the right effect to escape.

- Don't look back; focus on running forwards.

- Scream as loudly as you can.

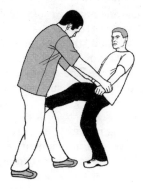

figure 5.5 double-hand grab (1)   **figure 5.6** double-hand grab (2)

Escapes from neck holds

Strangulation from the front

When an assailant places his hands around your neck and presses inwards on the side of your neck (a pincer-like action), this is called strangulation. A normal person will have between three to seven seconds to escape before being rendered unconscious. The action here is to effectively pull your neck free but, to be sure of success, use one of your arms as a lever. When your assailant grabs your neck (Figure 5.7) step back onto your left leg (Figure 5.8). Raise your right arm up high (Figure 5.9) and bring it over your head towards your left side (Figure 5.10), in an arc-like movement. As you do this, turn on the balls of your feet to your left turning both your shoulders and hips and the assailant's attack will cease. Kick your assailant in the groin (Figure 5.11) and run away.

Summary

- Step back

- Arm high up in the air

- Turn to the left

- Bring your arm down

- Escape

- Kick

- Run

Coaching points

- When you are strangled, tip your head down; it will help to alleviate the strangle.

- Don't panic; move fast; don't hesitate; you don't have long. About one and half seconds are wasted in thinking time, which leaves a minimum of only two seconds before you start feeling faint.

- Try to keep your hips and shoulders parallel throughout this technique.

- Think about the arc of a rainbow when bringing your arm over. The mechanical action should be at your assailant's wrist.

- Kick hard, use the kicking leg to step back and turn before running.

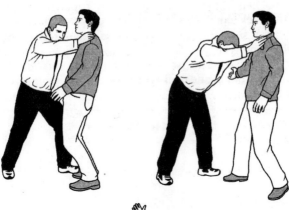

figure 5.7
front strangulation (1)

figure 5.8
front strangulation (2)

figure 5.9
front strangulation (3)

figure 5.10 front strangulation (4)

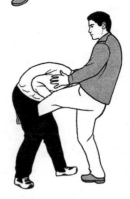

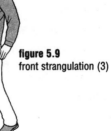

figure 5.11 front strangulation (5)

Strangulation from the rear

Being attacked from the rear can be very frightening and such a surprise attack can be disorientating. Compose yourself quickly. Step to the side and strike your assailant's groin with your cupped hand (Figure 5.12) and as your assailant moves consequential to your strike, swiftly move forwards (Figure 5.13). Turn round and kick your assailant (Figure 5.14) then run away fast.

Summary

- Strike groin

- Kick

- Run

Coaching points

- Remember to step to the side. This has the effect of making the strangle lopsided and your assailant will find it slightly more difficult to strangle you.

- Strike the groin with a cupped hand. Keep your hand relaxed and use a whipping action with the hand rather than a direct slapping action.

- Move away quickly, because your assailant's balance may bear down on you.

- If your assailant turns and falls, forget the kick, just run.

- When you kick, you might find it more effective to focus your kicking foot through your assailant's legs so your instep and shin are doing the damage, as opposed to the foot.

Note: the difference between a choke and strangulation

The two types of neck holds are the choke and the carotid strangle. The techniques of choking and strangulation differ greatly from each other although the end result is the same – loss of consciousness. Strangling, a pincer action of the neck, inhibits the blood flow to the brain. Choking, pressure to the windpipe, prevents air penetrating the lungs. The response to a choke will be the sensation of swallowing your tongue and gagging. The strangle will make you feel light-headed and weak at the knees causing you to fall. The choke is considered more dangerous because of the potential damage to the cartilage of the trachea (air passage). The combination of the choke and the strangle can be carried out by constricting the neck with a ligature.

figure 5.12 rear strangulation (1)   **figure 5.13** rear strangulation (2)

figure 5.14 rear strangulation (3)

Escape from the rear choke

This is another potentially dangerous attack, since, if the cartilage of your throat is damaged, it cannot be repaired. This attack will involve an assailant approaching from behind you and placing his right arm around the front of your neck (Figure 5.15). Pressure is then applied to your throat debilitating you in seconds. The issue here is to change the potentially damaging choke to a strangulation which is easier to manage, by pushing your assailant's elbow to a point under your chin (Figure 5.16). To make this easier, step back onto your right leg. Pinch the skin between your assailant's legs or strike to the groin (Figure 5.17). This will momentarily redirect his attention. Grab your assailant's hand with your left hand prising his arm from your neck. This will be easier after you have struck the assailant's groin. Step forwards onto your left leg (Figure 5.18). Turn around to face your assailant (Figure 5.19) and kick (Figure 5.20). Run away.

Summary

- Change the choke to a strangle
- Grab assailant's hand
- Step forwards and turn
- Kick
- Run

Coaching points

- This is another attack where your primary objective is to restore your ability to breathe. There are many methods to use to escape but this is by far the simplest and easiest to learn.

- As you step forwards, pull down on your assailant's elbow, pulling it towards your chest. In this situation, it is difficult for your assailant to recover and it also helps you regain your breath.

- Turn around quickly and deliver a kick to the groin or a knee strike to the body.

- Run away from the assailant to safety.

figure 5.15 rear choke (1)

figure 5.16 rear choke (2)

figure 5.17 rear choke (3)

figure 5.18 rear choke (4)

figure 5.19 rear choke (5)

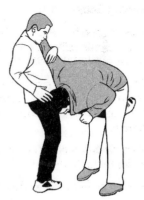

figure 5.20 rear choke (6)

Defence to side head chancery

This can be a very powerful hold and difficult to escape from. This is why assailants use it to control you. It involves an assailant placing an arm around your neck and holding you firmly using both arms (Figure 5.21). If the assailant is very strong you may need to redirect his attention by pinching the skin between the legs or striking their groin (Figure 5.22). To escape, place one hand on the front of the assailant's hip and the other on his bottom (Figure 5.23). Keep your chin tucked down, step back onto the left leg (Figure 5.24) and at the same time push with both hands against the hip joint to open up a space between the assailant's arms. Pop your head out from under your assailant's arm. Kick (Figure 5.25) and run.

Summary

- Strike or pinch (if necessary)

- Step back

- Push hip to escape

- Kick

- Run

Coaching points

- If your assailant has a very strong hold around your neck you must overcome this to escape. This will mean exerting some pain to your assailant by striking or pinching him where it's very painful (see Appendix 2 for points to attack).

- It will be vital to keep your chin close to your own chest in order to escape, otherwise if your assailant's arm is under your chin, it will be difficult to break free.

- Push your assailant's pelvis backwards as well as sideways away from you.

- Just as your assailant is regaining balance is the right time to kick. Kick the point on the lateral aspect of the thigh to deliver a dead leg. Your assailant will not be able to pursue you.

figure 5.21 head chancery from the side (1) **figure 5.22** head chancery from the side (2)

figure 5.23 head chancery from the side (3) **figure 5.24** head chancery from the side (4)

figure 5.25 head chancery from the side (5)

Defence to the throat grab

In this potentially dangerous situation, it is normal to try to grab your assailant's hands (Figure 5.26) while gasping for air. Be aware of the possibility that your assailant might strike you with his free hand. Lean slightly backwards (Figure 5.26) and then swiftly turn to your left pulling your assailant's thumb away from your throat (Figure 5.27). Quickly push your assailant (Figure 5.28) away from you and escape. Don't wait for a response... run!

Summary

- Grab the wrist

- Lean back

- Thumb off your neck

- Push down

- Run

Coaching points

- The important aspect of this technique is to quickly restore your ability to breathe.

- This technique is very simple but effective.

- Be very aware of an attack from your assailant's free hand.

- Push hard.

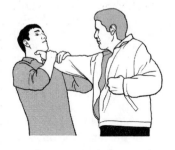 

figure 5.26 throat grab (1)   **figure 5.27** throat grab (2)

figure 5.28 throat grab (3)

Escapes from garrotting to the front and rear

When a ligature is placed around your neck, it can be extremely dangerous to you, because of the potential loss of consciousness. The ligature is normally placed around the neck with the strap ends crisscrossed over one another for efficiency. We are going to look at three versions of this: two from the front and one from the rear. When attacked from the front much will depend on which strap is on the top and your action will take one of two forms.

From the front: version 1

If your assailant uses a ligature to strangle you, it can be more vicious than using his hands (Figure 5.29). The ligature may dig into the skin, but don't panic. Determine which part of the ligature is on the top. If the right side of the ligature comes over the top, push your elbow down on top of your assailant's wrist (Figure 5.30) while you step back onto your left leg. This minimizes the use of the ligature by your assailant. Bend your knees – using your body weight in this manner (Figure 5.31) helps put your assailant off-balance. Strike your assailant's groin (Figure 5.32). Reach up and grab your assailant's head (Figure 5.33) and pull it downwards to escape (Figure 5.34). Push your assailant to the ground and then run.

Summary

- Push down with elbow
- Strike groin
- Grab assailant's head
- Push to ground
- Run

Coaching points

- Again, your primary objective is to restore your ability to breathe and then escape.
- As you push down with your elbow, allow the ligature to slide around your neck and at the same time push your other hand, now holding your assailant's hand, towards the assailant.
- When striking the groin use a flicking action.
- Reach up and grab the hair on the head. If the assailant is bald, grab the ears. A kick to the groin is optional.
- Remember to run **away** from the assailant and not in a direction in which they can easily pursue you.

figure 5.29 garrotting from the front: version 1 (1)

figure 5.30 garrotting from the front: version 1 (2)

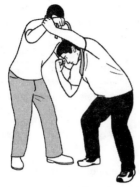

figure 5.31 garrotting from the front: version 1 (3)

figure 5.32 garrotting from the front: version 1 (4)

figure 5.33 garrotting from the front: version 1 (5)

figure 5.34 garrotting from the front: version 1 (6)

From the front: version 2

In this second variation, the left side of the ligature is on the top (Figure 5.35). Again, don't panic. Finding the left strap end uppermost, grab hold of your assailant's right wrist with your **left** hand (Figure 5.36) and place your right hand under your assailant's left elbow. Turn the assailant's arms in an anticlockwise direction to open up the ligature (Figure 5.36). Kick your assailant to the groin (Figure 5.37) and run in the opposite direction.

Summary

- Twist arms
- Escape
- Run
- Kick

Coaching points

- Again, your primary objective is to restore your ability to breathe and then escape.
- Using your body weight in the same way as in the previous technique is useful.
- Twist the ligature to open the strap so you can breathe.
- Keep your chin down.
- Kick hard and run away from your assailant.

figure 5.35 garrotting from the front: version 2 (1)

figure 5.36 garrotting from the front: version 2 (2)

figure 5.37 garrotting from the front: version 2 (3)

From the rear

The third variation is probably the most dangerous. You are attacked from a position behind you while the assailant wraps a ligature around your neck (Figure 5.38). **NEVER** step forward. Step back through your assailant's legs onto your left leg and strike the groin (Figure 5.39). Turn round and grab behind your assailant's knees (Figure 5.40). Pull the knees and at the same time push with your body to topple the assailant to the ground (Figure 5.41). Run!

Summary

- Step through legs
- Strike the groin
- Pull back of knees
- Run

Coaching points

- Never step forwards! This increases the effectiveness of the attack and shortens the time you'll be conscious.

- Step backwards into your assailant's space and strike the groin hard.

- This will cause your assailant to bend forwards at the waist and at the knees slightly.

- Exploit this and pull the knees towards you in a upwards direction while pushing against your assailant with your body. You'll be surprised at how little strength is needed to make this technique work effectively.

- A kick to the groin is optional but run away from your assailant's direction.

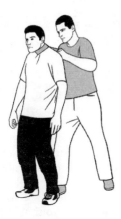 

figure 5.38 garrotting from the rear (1)   **figure 5.39** garrotting from the rear (2)

 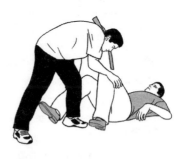

figure 5.40 garrotting from the rear (3)   **figure 5.41** garrotting from the rear (4)

Escapes from bear hugs to front and rear

In this situation there are four options depending on the way your assailant wraps his arms around you.

1 Arms over from the front

When you are grabbed by an assailant from the front, it is likely that he will be trying to lift you up. This situation will depend on the assailant placing his arms over yours (Figure 5.42). Before the assailant lifts you, place your hands on your assailant's thighs (Figure 5.43) and take a step back. This creates a space for you to lift your leg ready to strike your assailant to the groin (Figure 5.44). Your assailant will probably bend slightly forward consequential to the knee strike. Kick your leg through your assailant's legs and push down on your assailant's thighs (Figures 5.45) propelling the assailant to the ground. Kick to the groin (Figure 5.46) to prevent his chasing you and make good your escape.

Summary

- Step back

- Knee the groin

- Push down on the thighs

- Kick

- Run

Coaching points

- Be utterly determined to succeed.

- If your assailant has a very strong grip, bite the side of the neck hard.

- The knee strike will take your assailant by surprise so be ready for the next part.

- Push your assailant downwards and backwards and watch your own balance, particularly if your assailant holds on to you.

- Follow up with a kick to the groin. This kick is more of a stamping action than a flicking action of the foot.

- Be aware of where you are to run to.

figure 5.42 bear hug – arms over from the front (1)

figure 5.43 bear hug – arms over from the front (2)

figure 5.44 bear hug – arms over from the front (3)

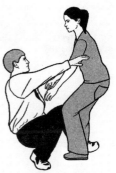

figure 5.45 bear hug – arms over from the front (4)

figure 5.46 bear hug – arms over from the front (5)

2 Arms under from the front

This time your assailant attacks you from the front by placing his arms around your body and under your arms (Figure 5.47). This leaves your arms free. Slap the ears hard (Figure 5.48) and then grab your assailant's hair (Figure 5.49) at the back of their head. If they are bald grab the ear. Pull the hair or ear to tilt the assailant's head fully backwards. Once in this position strike directly downwards on the nose (Figure 5.50) and the assailant will fall to the floor. Again, kick and run (as seen in Figure 5.46).

Summary

- Slap

- Pull hair

- Strike nose

- Kick

- Run

Coaching points

- If your assailant has a strong grip, push your thumbs into the space at the back of the ears.

- When slapping the ears, keep your hands slightly cupped.

- When striking the nose, make sure that you use the heel of the hand to strike the fleshy part of the nose near to the bridge. Strike downwards into the face and not upwards. At the very least this will have the effect of making the eyes water thereby making it difficult for your assailant to see you.

- Use a stamping action when kicking.

figure 5.47 bear hug – arms under from the front (1)

figure 5.48 bear hug – arms under from the front (2)

figure 5.49 bear hug – arms under from the front (3)

figure 5.50 bear hug – arms under from the front (4)

3 Arms over from the rear

This situation involves the assailant attacking you from a position behind you and placing his arms around your body and over your arms (Figure 5.51). It is very likely that your assailant will want to lift you, so the important thing here is to act swiftly. Place your hands on your own thighs and push with your elbows (Figure 5.52) against your assailant's arms. This will create a small space in front of you. Turn your right heel outwards (Figure 5.52) and turn your body to your left, inwards towards your assailant. Step back onto your left leg (Figure 5.53), ducking under your assailant's arms. Once free, kick your assailant (Figure 5.54) and run.

Summary

- Hands on thighs
- Turn foot
- Step back to escape
- Kick
- Run

Coaching points

- In this instance, if your assailant has a strong grip, kick backwards with your heels against his legs.

- Timing is important. The very moment you realize the arms are coming around you, lean forwards slightly and place your hands on your thighs.

- Push your hands downwards on your thighs and push your elbows forwards at the same time.

- Once you have a space, slip underneath and to the side. Sometimes it is useful to lift your arms to help you manoeuvre underneath.

- Once you are free, kick your assailant hard to prevent him following you when you run away.

figure 5.51 bear hug – arms over from the rear (1)

figure 5.52 bear hug – arms over from the rear (2)

figure 5.53 bear hug – arms over from the rear (3)

figure 5.54 bear hug – arms over from the rear (4)

4 Arms under from the rear

This situation involves the assailant attacking you from a position behind you and placing his arms around your body and under your arms (Figure 5.55). Again, you can be lifted, so the important thing, once again, is act swiftly. The moment you are grabbed, strike the back of your assailant's hands near to the wrist bones, to release the grip (Figures 5.56 and 5.57). Bend forwards and push your bottom against your assailant's leg. This will have the effect of preventing your assailant from grabbing you again as well as making space for you to escape. Grab your assailant's foot (Figure 5.58) and lift it up (Figure 5.59) while you maintain a slightly seated position. Your assailant will be thrown to the floor. Kick to the groin (Figure 5.60) and run.

Summary

- Strike hand
- Grab and lift the foot
- Kick
- Run

Coaching points

- If your assailant has a strong grip you can use your elbow to strike their face. However, the strike to the hand, if done properly, is very painful.
- Remember to sit down onto your assailant's leg by sticking your bottom out backwards behind you.
- Look down and you will see your assailant's foot begin to lift, toes first. At this moment, grab the heel and pull the foot upwards all the while sitting downwards. You are using your bottom as the fulcrum of a simple lever to topple your assailant.
- Again, when kicking, use a stamping action.

figure 5.55 bear hug – arms under from the rear (1)

figure 5.56 bear hug – arms under from the rear (2)

figure 5.57 bear hug – arms under from the rear (3)

figure 5.58 bear hug – arms under from the rear (4)

figure 5.59 bear hug – arms under from the rear (5)

figure 5.60 bear hug – arms under from the rear (6)

Escapes from hair grabs

When an assailant grabs your hair it gives them a distinct advantage. The assailant is able to determine the distance between you, making any follow-up attack easy. This attack can be perpetrated in one of two ways, either from in front of you or from behind you.

Hair pull from the front

To escape from this situation, you need to be just as determined as your assailant. You are attacked from a position in front of you and the assailant grabs your hair (Figure 5.61), pulling you forwards. Take a step backwards onto your left leg (Figure 5.62) to regain your balance and slap the assailant's forearm sharply (Figure 5.63). Move away from your assailant and make good your escape.

(**Note:** If your assailant grabs with his right hand then the direction of the slap must be to your left side. If the opposite is the case then simply reverse the technique.)

Summary

- Step back
- Slap
- Run

Coaching points

- This is the simplest way to defend yourself from this attack.

- When you slap the assailant's wrist, make sure that your hand is travelling in a direction parallel to your face. In this way, the technique works against the short extensors of your assailant's hand making it easy to escape.

- Again, a kick is optional.

figure 5.61 hair grab from the front (1)   **figure 5.62** hair grab from the front (2)

figure 5.63 hair grab from the front (3)

Hair pull from the rear

If attacked from behind, the first thing you will feel is your head being propelled backwards (Figure 5.64). Bend your knees (Figure 5.65) and look towards your assailant then deliver a sharp kick to your assailant's leg (Figure 5.66). Run.

Summary

- Step back
- Kick
- Run

Coaching points

- You can be caught off guard easily with this technique, so be alert.

- The moment you feel the attack, you will experience pain as your hair is pulled. Duck down and turn towards your assailant.

- Kick backwards to strike your assailant.

- Finally, run away from your assailant.

figure 5.64 hair grab from the rear (1)   **figure 5.65** hair grab from the rear (2)

figure 5.66 hair grab from the rear (3)

Defence while attacked on the ground

Being attacked while on the ground is possibly the scariest situation to be in. You will not have the leverage enjoyed when standing up. However, the following methods are very effective if carried out correctly. The problem with this situation is that you are at a distinct disadvantage. Whenever you find yourself knocked to the ground – get up fast.

Defence against kicks to the head and body while on the ground

In this example, the assailant will be kicking your head and body while you are lying on the ground. It may be that you are pushed to the ground or you stumble. Now you must defend yourself from this vulnerable position. One important point to make here is the way you should lie on the ground: to have a chance of success turn your body so that your feet point towards your assailant (Figure 5.67). When your assailant starts to kick you (Figure 5.68), lash out with both of your feet and legs (Figure 5.69) kicking your assailant's legs and groin. In our example, our victim has cleverly used one foot to block the kick while using his other to attack the assailant's groin (Figure 5.69). Continue to kick and lash out with your feet until you find a moment to get up. There is little point in competing in a kick-for-all while you are on the floor and your assailant is standing up. Get up and run.

Summary

- Lash out with kicks
- Get up
- Run

Coaching points

- Remember to orientate your feet towards your assailant.

- When your assailant comes into your range – your leg length – you can start lashing out and kicking with your legs. It doesn't matter where you hit your assailant. Try practising using one foot to block the assailant's kick while using your other to kick.

- Remember, your objectives are to get up and to run.

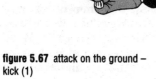

figure 5.67 attack on the ground –
kick (1)

figure 5.68 attack on the ground –
kick (2)

figure 5.69 attack on the ground –
kick (3)

Defence to strangle on the ground

This is a fairly typical attack if you are knocked to the ground. The assailant takes a superior position by sitting astride your chest while strangling you. The things you have to bear in mind here are that you have little space to move and that the leverage is not as good as if you were standing up. You are also limited as to how long you can spend escaping from this attack. Remember, you will have to move quickly and effectively.

When an assailant has manoeuvred on top of you bend your knees and bring your left foot over your assailant's right foot (Figure 5.70). Place your left hand on top of the assailant's right elbow and your right hand under the left elbow (Figure 5.71). Lift your bottom off the floor (Figure 5.72). This will have the effect of bringing your assailant's body weight forwards onto your neck, temporarily. When you sense this, immediately turn the elbow and your body to the left and your assailant will be tossed off you to a point on the left beside you (Figure 5.73). To ensure the assailant doesn't follow you, give a swift kick or strike to the groin. Roll backwards to stand up and escape by running away.

Summary

- Foot over
- Lift bottom
- Twist to left
- Kick
- Roll out and escape

Coaching points

- If you procrastinate or panic, you will quickly lose consciousness, so be alert and move swiftly.
- When twisting the arms it is always more beneficial to use the elbows as levers.
- Notice when you lift your bottom that your assailant's balance will be right above you and it is at this moment that you should roll them over to the side.
- Roll backwards away from your assailant to escape.

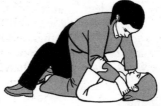

figure 5.70 attack on the ground –
strangulation (1)

figure 5.71 attack on the ground –
strangulation (2)

figure 5.72 attack on the ground –
strangulation (3)

figure 5.73 attack on the ground –
strangulation (4)

Rape scenario

How the situation starts is not important – how it is dealt with is. The vital point to make here is the female should make it clear that she says and means no (Figure 5.74) and her body language should support that. In our scenario, the female is knocked to the ground and the assailant then manoeuvres between her legs (Figure 5.75). Waste no time. Lift your knees (Figure 5.76) and gouge your assailant's eyes (Figure 5.77). Bring your knees together and kick violently and repetitively at your assailant's chest (Figure 5.78) propelling the assailant backwards (Figure 5.79). Do not remain lying down.

Summary

- Lift knees
- Gouge eyes
- Kick
- Run, shout and scream

Coaching points

- Irrespective of how the scenario starts, be alert to what possibilities may ensue.
- Send out the right signals – say and mean **NO**.
- The very moment your assailant comes close enough, gouge the eyes with your thumbs and bring your knees up to begin kicking.
- Once your assailant is off you, do not hesitate. Get up immediately and run away from your assailant, shouting and screaming.

figure 5.74 rape simulation (1)

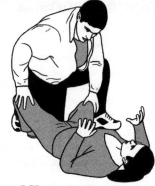

figure 5.75 rape simulation (2)

figure 5.76 rape simulation (3)

figure 5.77 rape simulation (4)

figure 5.78 rape simulation (5)

figure 5.79 rape simulation (6)

Technical considerations

This section will help you develop a deeper and broader understanding of how everything fits together. 'A little knowledge is a dangerous thing' and therefore supplementing your current level of knowledge with detail will help you understand more of what you are doing and why. This is important because ultimately you will have to justify your actions if an instance is brought before a judge (Chapter 06 gives more detail).

Anatomy of the body

The body has many weaknesses. Articulations or joints allow movement of the body and it is these very articulations that give the body sites of weakness. It takes a weight of only seven to ten lbs to dislocate a joint, which can cause extreme pain and, more importantly, could even cause the loss of function of that limb. It takes even less effort to damage or dislocate fingers.

Some weak points are called **vital points** and others **pressure points** (sites where a nerve or blood vessel crosses over a bony part close to the surface of the skin). See Figure 5.80. It is very difficult to locate pressure points accurately and from a self defence perspective there is little point in wasting time trying to find these points if you are attacked. Vital points represent parts of the body where it is easy to strike and cause an effect. It will be useful to explore this further and find where these points (detailed in Appendix 2) are on your own body.

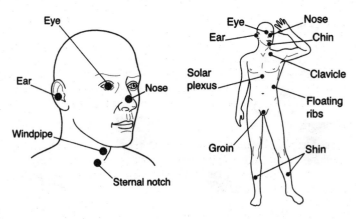

figure 5.80 vital points of the head and body

Gravity is your friend – if you can push or pull your assailant off balance, you gain an advantage. Learning how to put someone off balance and then toppling them to the floor can be quite a difficult technique but it can be very productive learning these methods to enhance your basic skills. They are known as throws. There are only very elementary throws in this book's basic programme of self defence.

Use of visualization

This will become very useful to you when you begin to practise the physical protocols. Visualization is basically a form of mental practice. When you see yourself perform the skill it is known as **internal imagery**. When you imagine how someone else might perform the skill it is known as **external imagery**. The process is similar to playing a video on the inside of your forehead and watching the action. It can be slowed down or freeze framed by you. It is a way you can use your mind as a tool towards achieving something new or improving something already known. Imagery simply helps you focus on a specific task and sets up the mental responses to carry it through. The process of mentally 'going through the motions' works hand in hand with physical practice to turn this chapter's protocols into near reflexes.

Types of attacker

Assailants can be categorized according to their behavioural traits. This is useful for us as it brings some sense to the different types of attack that may be perpetrated on us.

The opportunist

The typical opportunist has no plan. Whenever a situation and the opportunity arise, they take the chance to do whatever they do. The word chance is used here deliberately. There is a possibility of getting caught and it may be the rush of adrenalin that attracts this type of person to behave in this way.

The mugger

This describes a person who is prepared to use violence to achieve his crime. They will perpetrate their crime any time, any where. Theft is usually their motive and they do not view assault or violence adversely.

The professional

They plan everything in fine detail. They investigate the scene and their prey to find out every little detail to give them a major advantage. More often than not a professional will want to use minimum force and escape easily. They treat what they do as both a science and a game with the law enforcement authorities.

What happens during an attack

Fighting for a wristwatch, a necklace, a credit card or a couple of pounds is certainly not worth the bodily harm you could incur during a fight with an assailant. Remember that everything you own can be repurchased, **your life and your health cannot.**

By incorporating my suggestions for safety into your daily routine, you can decrease the possibility of having to defend yourself physically. Property is **never** worth losing your life for. There are basically three strategies employed in self defence:

1 Eliminate danger when in the home or at work, on the street or in your car.
2 Learn to recognize and avoid dangers; running, talking and screaming are particularly useful.
3 Fight only when your life or your health is in danger. The only expectation is, if you **have** to fight, fight hard. Do only that which you have to escape and then run.

During a real attack everything will go haywire. Most of us have had some physical altercation during our lives. Attacks are situations which the mind either colours or denies. Our view on the use of violence will colour the event. After the event we may say we were 'appalled' or 'fought courageously', despite what happened in reality. As a defence mechanism we tend to block out of our minds the pain associated with the incident. For those who have never had such an altercation, here is what happens.

Adrenalin will rush into the stomach and set off a **fight or flight** mechanism. This is a physiological reaction in which the body releases a sudden burst of energy in anticipation of either fighting or running away. Effectively, the muscular system demands additional oxygen and salts and the transport system (blood) is increased to meet this demand. Consequently, blood held in the digestive system is redirected to the muscles. Adrenalin is pumped into the stomach causing the fluttering in your stomach known as butterflies. This is actually a series of small contractions to ensure that blood is moved to the muscles and does not stay in the digestive organs. Some people have reported a shivering effect as well and this is caused by the increase of local blood flow in the muscle and the twitching of fibres preparing for a full contraction.

The eyes are the primary source of information for most of us, and yet few appreciate or know how the eyes work and how best to optimize their use. The eyes have two main fields of vision, namely an objective field and peripheral field. The objective field is a very narrow field and specific to the focus of any object we look at directly. The peripheral vision includes the area around the objective vision which is not directly used to look at anything specifically but from which we derive a great deal of information (see Figure 5.81). The objective field provides us with specific information on what we are looking at directly and the peripheral field provides us with the information on what else is happening around us. Mostly the information in the peripheral field is slightly blurred but it still readily detects movement.

Your eyes give away a great deal of information too. Normally people will look objectively at their target before hitting it. Not doing this is a telltale sign of anyone who has experience in fighting. Consider the boxer who ducks and sways to avoid his gaze fixing on any part of his opponent. This way he can pick a target without telegraphing his intention.

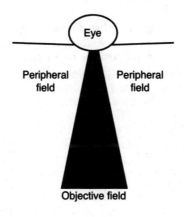

figure 5.81 range of eye vision

Use of the peripheral field can be of great value for improving awareness of the environment around you. Consider an attack to the head with a fist. Instead of looking directly at the fist, which involves many different processes in the brain attempting to determine distance, speed of attack, etc. use your peripheral field of vision to detect it. You can instinctively raise your hand to block the attack while looking directly at your attacker and still see the fist being blocked. Range of vision is very important. In a physically violent encounter we resort to using our objective vision. This is known as visual tunnelling. In order to see a wider field we must learn to use our peripheral range. Day in, day out we use our peripheral vision for a whole range of things, but it seems whenever we engage in combat we suffer from visual tunnelling. This is a natural reflex, a phenomenon which has the effect of drawing the peripheral range inwards, thus limiting your range of vision. It is as if we are looking through a glass tube. All you see clearly is what is at the very end of the tube, with everything else around it being blurred or obscured.

After the event the body may still be experiencing the fight or flight mechanism, although any shivering is likely to be due to shock rather than preparation for further action. The sudden reduction of adrenalin in the digestive system and the restoration of normal blood flow cause our memory and attentions to be distracted, making it difficult to recall details of recent events.

Chaos and fear

Some people have reported that a sense of panic and shock has caused them to freeze to the spot. The chaos, shock, speed, confusion, terror and viciousness of an attack can all cause an inducement of fear and a person can, almost literally, be seen to freeze. Through practice, you'll learn to develop a sense of strength, grace and balance in such situations. It is essential to aim towards a maximum flow of contact between you and your attacker. By keeping close contact with your attacker you are in a better position to respond to changes in action and still have a moderate amount of control over the situation. Also, avoid fixing the situation in any one place; keep things moving to prevent your attacker being able to overcome you.

Keeping your distance – zones and personal space

There are three zones or distances we maintain between people (see Figure 5.82). It is important to understand this so that you can take the appropriate action depending on which zone your attacker is in. The closer the attacker is to you does not necessarily increase the danger but it can limit your ability to fight back.

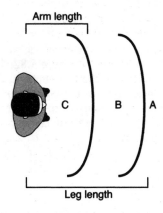

figure 5.82 comfort zones and personal space

Intimate (tertiary) zone

This is zone C in Figure 5.82. Only allow people you trust into this zone. This is difficult to control since in the modern world we must allow others we would rather keep out of the intimate zone to invade our space, for example on a train, a bus, a tram or in a lift. It is a very personal zone and, consequently, here you are extremely vulnerable to attack. Moreover, persons moving in and out of this zone at their will can make you feel very uncomfortable because you appear have no control over their actions.

Personal (secondary) zone

This is zone B in Figure 5.82. It represents the space in which you are comfortable with most people, and is normally associated as being at arm's length. If anyone should attack you in an unprovoked manner, in this zone you may be able to fend it off simply by stepping back out of the way.

Social (primary) zone

This is zone A in Figure 5.82 and is the distance represented by the length of your leg. When an attack occurs in this zone, it may be clearer to you because the aggressor will have to make up a greater distance to reach you, thereby giving you slightly more time to decide and act. An attacker will want to close down this area and get close to you before they make any attack. This makes it easier to perpetrate the act so beware of any strangers ingratiating themselves with you.

Territorial supremacy is another way of looking at our personal space instead of the ABC zones in Figure 5.82. This involves our belongings, be they in the kitchen, bathroom, car or the office. Others may only use articles belonging to you with your permission and when this occurs without permission, we may react violently. This is also covered by law through the Trespass Act forbidding unauthorized persons to walk on land not belonging to them across which there is no public access.

Shout and seek

Our attention is conditioned to be directed to screams for help. When escaping from any situation, scream at the top of your voice. Run for space particularly where there are people. Do not find yourself trapped in a confined space. Most large cities have CCTV networks around major routes. Familiarize yourself with the position of these cameras and if you need to walk to or from any destination consider planning your route to coincide with the cameras. Should you be attacked there is a better chance that it will be caught on camera.

Observations

Developing the ability to discern or interpret what one sees will certainly be a distinct advantage. With good observation skills it is possible to see an attack and respond to it before it overwhelms you. One useful observation technique is to learn the 'trigger strategy' for each attack. A typical example of a trigger strategy is revealed when an assailant is about to attack you. His body will tell you what is happening as he prepares his attack: when about to throw a punch, body weight will change position, breathing will change, the objective vision will be fixed to name but a few.

Summary

It is said that understanding something is more than 50% of the learning. The protocols in this book are easy to learn and their simplicity takes advantage of biomechanical superiority sourced from leverage. If you procrastinate it can be very difficult to get yourself out of a situation; it's much easier not to get yourself into one. If life were only that simple!

This book is not aimed at turning you into a 'have a go hero'. Rather, the opposite. It reinforces the intention of walking away or talking your way out of a situation, instead of becoming involved physically. However, the clear message is: if you need to engage in physical self defence, fight hard, then escape. There are many variables and fighting should only be a last resort to escape from a potentially dangerous situation.

Remember, we are all subject to the law of the land and none of us is above the law. The use of excessive force may find you accused of a crime of violence. The law provides that you may use only 'reasonable and necessary force' (see Chapter 06) to extricate yourself from a situation in which you are forced to use your skills.

We cannot control if and when we are going to be attacked, so the only things we can rely on are our skills, abilities and understanding. Having learned the techniques in this book, you should feel more prepared and able should the ugly spectre of attack descend on you.

06

the law and you

In this chapter you will learn:
- what the law says about self defence
- about reasonable force
- what to do if you are accused of excessive force.

Many people worry about hurting others by using excessive force when defending themselves. They are also concerned about being arrested and charged, not to mention the consequential court appearance. It is important to know just what the law says you may and may not do in these situations so that you can stand up for your rights with the law behind you, as opposed to against you.

It is vital to distinguish the difference between what is physically **possible** during a hostile physical encounter and what is permitted by law. The correct approach should be to use a technique aimed to prevent your aggressor from attacking you. Using the wrong technique may result in you being in the dock facing charges of assault, rather than your assailant. Learned masters would agree that there is no point whatsoever, after successfully blocking an attack, in following through with either repetitive counterattacks or vicious strikes when a simple technique would suffice. True refinement seeks simplicity. This is the exact point where you can become legally unstuck. It is all too easy for the victim who initially only used self defence to protect himself from more serious injury to later become the aggressor by overreacting and using unnecessary force on his assailant.

The letter of the law varies between Scotland, England, Wales and Northern Ireland, just as it does between the various states of the US. Do not worry. Wherever you are, the law is dealing with the same type of problems and is designed to protect you. If attacked, use minimal force to make good your escape – and the law will be on your side.

In this chapter, we will look at the legal definitions involved in most self defence scenarios.

Definitions of assault

Assault is a common law crime and is generally defined as *every attack directed to take effect physically on the person of another... whether or not actual injury is inflicted. There must be criminal intent: an accidental injury, even although caused by a mischievous act does not amount to assault. It is not necessary that the attack should take effect in order to constitute this crime.* This is what constitutes an assault, although there are also specific statutes that deal with certain 'specialized' forms of attack. Assaults can be categorized into three groups:

1 menaces or intimidation
2 simple assaults
3 aggravated assaults.

Menaces and intimidation are basically threats of violence. Verbal threats are not deemed sufficient to be a crime of this sort, but threatening gestures, with or without verbal threats, would be sufficient. An example of this might be as follows:

> Eck, the local bully-boy, is standing on a street corner and it's your misfortune to be walking in his direction. As you get nearer he steps out to bar your way and prevents you from going any further. He states that unless you co-operate with him on some later date he will smash your skull into tiny fragments. While brandishing his large fearsome clenched fist under your nose, he goes on to tell you that he could tie you in knots, break all your bones and bust your nose.

This is a typical example of menacing or intimidation. It's the **threatening gesture**, not the spoken words, that constitute the assault.

Simple assaults include all minor attacks such as slaps, kicks and punches. These attacks can be considered dangerous just because of the consequential injuries capable of being inflicted on a victim. These assaults are classified as 'simple' because of the simplicity of the attack and not, in any way, due to the actual or likely results of the assault. There are, of course, many variations on this type of assault, common examples being a push to the chest or a slap in the face. Consider this scenario:

> You are at a private function and until now have been enjoying yourself, but a person you do not know has had a bit too much to drink and begins to pester you. You attempt to ignore him and change your seat. Despite this, the nuisance follows and continues in the annoying manner in which he started. You mingle with the crowd and make a conscious effort to avoid him, but by now the nuisance is becoming irate and frustrated. Eventually he decides that he is not to be made out as a fool. He then pushes you forward from behind and as you turn round he swings a punch at you.

This is a very typical situation. If someone is going to strike you then it will most probably be with this type of attack or a blatant unprovoked attack without warning. These pointless, but all too common, attacks can do untold damage if they meet their targets.

Although every attack can be dangerous, the more potentially dangerous attacks can be categorized as aggravated assaults. The attacks referred to here are by more than one person or attacks with weapons, the latter usually being the more dangerous type of attack.

An aspect of psychology may enter into aggravated attacks: the fear of how strongly the recipient will respond leads the aggressor to use a weapon. In the criminal mind, the act about to be perpetrated at that moment is more important than anything else and in their mind the weapon ensures success. This is indicative of a gross insecurity problem and a lack of self-respect. Similarly, a lack of self-confidence is displayed in multiple attacker incidents where it is unlikely that the assault would have taken place at all, had the individuals involved not been able to draw confidence from one another.

While en route from work to home you have to pass through a shopping precinct. You are accosted by a group of three thugs and to avoid any confrontation you move to the other side of the walkway. They follow and within seconds you are surrounded by the group members. You notice that one of them is holding a knife and another is holding a piece of wood. They begin to move towards you, brandishing their weapons, and launch an attack. First, the thug with the piece of wood pokes you in the stomach. You double up in pain and now the knife man puts his blade under your chin and by upward pressure you are forced to stand up. The last unarmed thug sinks his foot into your groin. You fall to the ground and having repeatedly kicked you to the body they depart, leaving you in extreme agony.

Very nasty; thugs like these don't muck around and the victim can be badly hurt.

Consider the options

Let's examine the three situations just described, and look at possible courses of action open to the victims. In the first situation the local bully-boy made a verbal threat, but not quite enough to prove a substantive crime of threat or menace.

Remember that old saying, *sticks and stones may break my bones but names will never harm me*. However, by brandishing his fist under your nose the assault was constituted. It was this threatening gesture that constituted the assault and it would be competent to say that the crime was now complete. The action open to you would vary according to your nature, but irrespective of your personality, passive or aggressive, you should endeavour to talk your way out first – remember those communication skills. This situation is a technical assault and not a bodily attack on your person. You would not therefore be justified in using force against the aggressor. If he advanced his threat and actually used violence then you would be justified in defending yourself physically.

Pre-emptive strike

There is a school of thought which states that a pre-emptive strike is a valuable form of self defence. With the pre-emptive strike, the burden of proof will be on you to prove that you had no other means of escape and believed that using any less force would have resulted in serious injury or death. You will need to have demonstrated that your escape by various means was not possible to prove that your physical response was justified. Lord Griffiths (1998) ruled that: *A person about to be attacked does not have to wait for his assailant to strike the first blow or fire the first shot, circumstance may justify a pre-emptive strike.* The key part of this ruling must be the belief that you are about to be attacked. Be sure you read **all** the signs correctly before you act recklessly.

Reasonable force

While the law provides that you do have a legal right to use **all reasonable and necessary force**, don't become a violent criminal. Maintain your sense of decency, know what is reasonable and be sure that your response was necessary. The law recognizes that sometimes it is necessary to resort to violence to preserve safety, but this is bound by certain legal and moral restrictions. If you do seriously injure someone then you have a moral responsibility to summon medical assistance and even give first aid, provided it does not put you in further danger. Remember that fighting (combat between two or more consenting persons both of whose goal it is to win) is illegal.

In our second situation, things were rather different. The attacker actually swung a punch, his target being your face, and in view of the circumstances this was a clear physical attack on you. The action you could take is quite simple. A deflection or block to parry or prevent the blow connecting is all that is required to fulfil the legal requirement of self defence. In order to prevent a further attack on you one good hard punch to the solar plexus or a swift kick to the groin might suffice as an effective follow-up. This retaliation is capable of weakening the largest of men, but if you persist in multiple follow-up techniques you will find this action will have gone beyond mere self defence and become a revenge attack.

The final situation was an aggravated assault and there is no doubt that a substantive assault took place. Your potential action in these circumstances would be slightly more complex. The odds are stacked against you and there is a real danger to life and limb. The attacker with the piece of wood should be the first to be dealt with and when he pokes you in the stomach with the stick it should be possible for you to disarm him. If the thug with the knife knows how to use the weapon he will probably taunt you into making the first move against him, but possibly he will take the initiative and lunge forward, thrusting the knife towards you. Use the stick to strike him on the head. Having defeated the two armed thugs, it's possible that the third man may flee, but if he is made of of sterner stuff you may have to re-assess the situation and act with common sense. If he persists in his attack then use any technique that is going to have the desired effect of stopping the assault. Your action must be **consistent with common sense**. If you injure someone badly, you have a duty to summon assistance. Know when to stop and avoid becoming the assailant. If you don't lose your humanity and you don't give in to outrage, panic, fear or anger, you will know when to stop. Let common sense and humanity guide you. Fight as hard as you need to and stop when it's over. It is easy to hurt someone and difficult to know just how much to hurt them. A likely problem you may encounter is, rather than avoiding the use of excessive force, mustering enough force to halt an attacker. It is important to get into the right frame of mind from the onset. This should be borne out by fact and you should be in no doubt as to your position. With that in mind you need not worry about courtrooms and lawyers. Behave reasonably and only use reasonable force.

Who determines what is and what is not reasonable force? During an attack, you alone must determine this. Your decisions should be rational; do not allow the heat of the blood to overrule your decision-making process. It is easy to say this but very difficult to make happen. Keeping a cold head when under pressure takes intense training. When the attack is over it will be the courts that will decide whether your decision was a correct one. There is no such thing as minimum force, every situation will be different and judged on its merits and circumstances. Reasonable force is also difficult to determine or define and many facets or circumstances and merits must be considered when judging force to be reasonable. Just because you have the ability to carry out a particular technique, doesn't mean you have to.

In judging how much force to use one should consider:

- the gravity of the attack
- what other means are possible
- whether you are ready to use or indeed if you tried to use these means
- the size and strength of the parties involved
- the potential extent of injuries.

Despite the fact that our country provides a police force, there is only one person ultimately responsible for your personal safety – **YOU**. Take sensible measures in your protection, for example avoid dangerous people and places.

Legal position

The judicial system (post-assault) does not always do justice. In the case of Priestnall v Cornish (1969) the defendant was driving with his girlfriend in a Ford Cortina when he was involved in an incident with a Hillman Imp containing three men. The latter vehicle chased the defendant, overtook him on two occasions and braked sharply in front of him each time. Eventually, after a chase, both vehicles stopped and the drivers got out and faced each other in a somewhat aggressive mood. The defendant, who was genuinely frightened by the occupants of the other car, took hold of a Krooklock, and threatened by this, the others retreated into the Hillman Imp. The unfortunate defendant was subsequently charged with assault but was found not guilty on the grounds of self defence. The Prosecution appealed against this decision and at the higher court it was held that since the victim had retreated into his vehicle he could no longer be said to have posed a threat to the defendant who had ample opportunity to enter his car and drive off. The defence of self defence was not therefore applicable to this case. The *Criminal Law Review*, commenting on this case, stated that only in exceptional circumstances would an attack on a person who is retreating be held as self defence. The force used must be necessary, or seem to be necessary, for the defendant to protect himself or another from injury.

If you find yourself in a situation when you have used force, the police may become involved in an investigation. If you felt the level of force used by you was justified you must **state**, post-attack, that you honestly believed this to be so. When giving your account of the circumstances – **TELL THE TRUTH**. Do not embellish the truth to make yourself look good. It is quite common for people not to be able to remember much detail post-attack, although most people have a clear recollection of events. Time distorts memories. This is one reason why the police will want to know what you have experienced and witnessed as soon after the event as possible, notwithstanding that catching the criminal is of prime importance. If you deviate or exaggerate your statement to the police, you may become unstuck quickly as your account is compared to that of other witnesses and perhaps CCTV. This will not bode well for you as your credibility will come into question. It is always best to tell the truth as you see it from the onset. If you are arrested, the police are legally bound to make you aware that any response given by you to their questioning may be used as evidence. Being arrested is not the same as facing charges. Often police arrest everyone involved then sort the matter out afterwards. This is used as a method to quell the situation and separate parties rather than denying anyone their freedom. You will be entitled to legal representation and if you have to appear before a judge, a magistrate, etc. you are advised to have legal counsel. You can arrange this yourself or the police can do this if you are held in custody.

In 1980, Professor (Sir) Gerald Gordon (Scots Law) commented: *Whether or not a person can legally defend themself when attacked is open to question and must depend on the circumstances of each case.* He is of the opinion that: *A person attacked by a felon is probably not now entitled to stand his ground and defend himself if escape is open.* He points out, however, that the means of escape must be reasonable and states that *If for instance a victim could have jumped from a window to avoid his assailant he would only be expected to do so if this action did not in itself carry a risk of injury.*

There is another popular theory that when accosted you must take to your heels and run. While this might be good advice, on some occasions the law views things somewhat differently. The popular view is that many people think that by law you are required to disengage, withdraw, or temporize if at all possible. You are not. This is not factual. The modern law of self defence was set out by Lord Widgery in the 1969 case of Regina v Julien: *It is not, as we understand it, the law that a person threatened must take to his heels and run... but what is necessary is that he should demonstrate that he is prepared to temporize and disengage and perhaps to make some physical withdrawal.*

This is considered to be reasonable action. Failing to disengage or temporize when one can do so could be construed that a victim had the opportunity to escape but had the intention to stay to wreak revenge. The law here is clear: defend yourself using necessary and reasonable force, temporize, disengage and escape. If an assailant is badly injured as a consequence of your actions then you have an obligation to summon medical attention for the assailant, provided that it doesn't place you in further danger. Obviously any retaliation allegedly made in self defence must not be excessive. Lord Keith, in HMA v Docherty (1945), gave the eminently reasonable opinion that: *Some allowance must be made for the excitement or state of fear or the heat of the blood.*

Remember that self defence involves repelling an attack to protect yourself or another. The goal is to escape. Create an opportunity to escape and then exploit that opportunity. **Fight only if there is no other way out.**

Offensive weapons

NEVER carry weapons: it is against the law. Moreover, in a physically hostile situation, they can be used against you by those who would attack you. There are many advertisements and articles in magazines suggesting that carrying mace sprays, etc. to protect yourself is effective. It is not. In the majority of the cases where these sprays have been involved the victims have ended up spraying themselves because the flow of the spray is not clear and, regrettably, in that situation it's the last thing you'd think of. Police who carry sprays and gas canisters are trained in their use.

Don't carry knuckledusters, coshes, bike chains, knives or any other such weapon. If you drop it, it will be used against you. It can be taken from you and used against you too. Neither situation is encouraging. Carrying any such implement will be considered as an offensive weapon, irrespective of whether you intend to use it or not. You must have a very good justification for carrying an offensive weapon and the method of carrying will help underpin your intention. If you had a cleaver in your pocket, you'd find it very difficult to justify this. However, if it were securely wrapped and you were en route to deliver it to the blacksmith for repair or en route home from work, it might well be different. Every circumstance will be considered on its merits.

Summary

The law of the land does not offer you a carte blanche to protect yourself. It's not an exact science, but it's the only form of regulation we have to control society. It is vital to be able to physically protect yourself, your friends and family in the instance of unprovoked attack and equally vital that the law recognizes and permits this. The parameters for the use of force in self defence are not set in stone and every instance will be judged on the circumstances. Make sure you act reasonably and within the confines of the law to give yourself its additional protection. Lose your cool and overreact and you may find yourself facing charges. Keep a steady head and always act reasonably. Be a decent human being.

taking it further

Where to get further help

Women and children

Women's Aid:

England www.womensaid.org.uk
Scotland www.scottishwomensaid.co.uk
Ireland www.womensaid.ie
Northern Ireland www.niwaf.org
Wales www.welshwomensaid.org

Kidscape
2 Grosvenor Gardens
London SW1W 0DH
Tel: 020 7730 3300
Fax: 020 7730 7081
Helpline: 08451 205 204
www.kidscape.org.uk

Childline
0800 1111
www.childline.org.uk

Children 1st
83 Whitehouse Loan
Edinburgh EH9 1AT
Tel: 0131 446 2300
Fax: 0131 446 2339
www.children1st.org.uk

Rape Crisis centres

UK

www.rapecrisisscotland.org.uk
www.rapecrisis.org.uk/members.html

US

www.rainn.org/counseling-centers/index.html

Marriage guidance counselling

UK

www.relate.org.uk
www.professionalcounselling.co.uk/relationship_couple_
counselling.html

US

www.keepyourmarriage.com
www.okmarriage.org/Services/MarriageGuidance.asp

US civil rights

www.acri.org
www.legal-definitions.com/civil-rights-law/

The Suzy Lamplugh Trust
National Centre for Personal Safety
Hampton House
20 Albert Embankment
London SE1 7TJ
Tel: 020 7091 0014
Fax: 020 7091 0015
www.suzylamplugh.org

Andrea Adams Trust
www.andreaadamstrust.org

Society as a whole

The Samaritans
The Upper Mill Kingston Road,
Ewell
Surrey KT17 2AF
Tel: 020 8394 8300
Fax: 020 8394 8301
www.samaritans.org.uk

Citizens Advice Bureau
www.citizensadvice.org.uk

Commission on Racial Equality
www.cre.gov.uk

The law

The Law Society

Scotland
26 Drumsheugh Gardens
Edinburgh EH3 7YR
Tel: 0131 226 7411
Textphone: 0131 476 8359
Fax: 0131 225 2934
www.lawscot.org.uk

England and Wales
General enquiries tel: 020 7242 1222
www.lawsociety.org.uk

The Health & Safety Executive
HSE Infoline tel: 0845 345 0055
www.hse.gov.uk

Sports councils

UKSPORT
Home Countries Sports
Council
40 Bernard Street
London
WC1N 1ST
Tel: 020 7211 5100

England
Sport England·
3rd Floor Victoria House
Bloomsbury Square
London WC1B 4SE
Tel: 08458 508 508
Fax: 020 7383 5740

Ireland
Irish Sports Council
Top Floor, Block A
Westend Office Park
Blanchardstown,
Dublin 15, Ireland
Tel: +353 1 8608800

Sports Council for NI
House of Sport
Upper Malone Road
Belfast BT9 5LA
Tel: 028 90 381222
Fax: 028 90 682757

Scotland
Sportscotland
Caledonia House
South Gyle
Edinburgh EH12 9DQ
Tel: 0131 317 7200

Wales
Sports Council for Wales
Sophia Gardens
Cardiff CF11 9SW
Tel: 029 2033 8200
Fax: 029 2030 0600

Local sports councils
Contact your district or county council or local authority who can provide you with a listing for each local sports council.

Other bodies

British Telecom Malicious Call Bureau 0800 661 441

Emergency services
In the UK, dial 999.
In the US, dial 911.
In Europe, dial 112 (also the international emergency number for GSM phones).

Police forces
Each police force will have a community education and community liaison department. Contact your local police headquarters.

Scottish Ju Jitsu Association
3 Dens Street, Dundee DD4 6BU
Tel: 01382 458262
www.scottish-jujitsu.com

Additional websites

Backpacking and hitchhiking
www.hikingandbackpacking.com
www.backpacking.net

Body Language
www.changingminds.org

Bullying
www.bullying.co.uk

appendix 1: your rights

The following are an illustration of human and social rights – in my words. You may have further legal rights not covered here and to find these out see p. 133.

- The right to decide how to lead your life, including pursuit of your own goals and dreams and establishing your own priorities.
- The right to your own values, beliefs, opinions and emotions – and the right to respect yourself for them, no matter what the opinion of others.
- The right to tell others how you wish to be treated, including the common rights to be treated like a human being.
- The right to express yourself and to say, 'No', 'I don't know', 'I don't understand', or even 'I don't care'. You have the right to take the time you need to formulate your ideas before expressing them.
- The right to ask for information or help – without having negative feelings about your needs.
- The right to change your mind, to make mistakes and to sometimes act illogically with full understanding and acceptance of the consequences.
- The right to like yourself even though you're not perfect and sometimes do less than you are capable of doing as well as the right to excel and reach your full potential.
- The right to have positive, satisfying relationships within which you feel comfortable and free to express yourself honestly – and the right to change or end relationships if they don't meet your needs.

- The right to change, enhance or develop your life in any way you determine.

This list is neither exhaustive nor exclusive but an illustration of the main rights we all have.

Vital points of the body

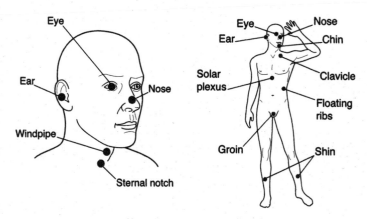

figure 5.80 vital points of the head and body

Body part	How to strike it	Effect
Eyes	Use your finger or thumb to poke into the eye	Temporary loss of sight
Ears	Strike the ear with a partially cupped hand	This percussive blow will disorientate
Nose	Strike the nose with your palm heel	Makes the eyes water or damages the nasal septum

Windpipe	Compress the windpipe with your forearm or hand or squeeze with your fingers	Can induce unconsciousness
	Strike the windpipe with the side of your hand	Can induce unconsciousness and damage to the windpipe
Clavicle	Strike with the bottom of a clenched fist or hand	Produces a great deal of pain and if broken immobilises the corresponding arm
Solar plexus	Strike this with either the bottom of your fist or with the knuckles	Temporary loss of breath
Floating ribs	Strike these ribs from the side with an elbow or hand or knee	Temporary loss of breath but possibility of serious systemic damage if the ribs break
Groin	Strike the genitals with the hand, or foot or knee	Temporary debilitation

Useful pressure points of the body

This list is not exhaustive but includes points that are easily accessible and effective.

Point	How to attack it	Effect
Behind the ear	Press thumbs or fingers into the space behind the ear and in front of the occipital bone	Extreme pain and disorientation
Facial cheeks	Press your thumbs or fingers into the cheeks near to the wisdom teeth	Excruciating pain
Nose	Push against the philtrum or the nasal septum with the palm of your hand	Will make eyes water

Windpipe	Compress the windpipe with your forearm or hand or squeeze with your fingers	Can induce unconsciousness
Sternal notch	Push your finger into the sternal notch and press downwards	Searing pain
Shin	Strike with the knee or the foot	Pain and loss of ability to stand up

index

DATE DUE